SO-BNV-048

Student Guide

To Ideas and Patterns in Literature III

IDEAS AND PATTERNS IN LITERATURE III *is an anthology which explores recurring themes, ideas, and forms in literature. The anthology itself contains only the literature, with a few brief introductions and connecting headnotes. All of the study material — comments, biographies, and questions — appears in this separate* Student Guide. *This arrangement is designed to make your study of literature more enjoyable.*

— The Editors

THE AUTHORS

*Edgar H. Knapp, Associate Professor of English
and Education at The Pennsylvania State University,
has taught in secondary schools and is
author of* Introduction to Poetry.

*Ralph J. Wadsworth is Director of English
at the Glastonbury Public Schools in
Glastonbury, Connecticut. He has also served on the
Advisory Council to
the Connecticut Commissioner of Education.*

GENERAL EDITORS

*William G. Leary and Dr. Knapp
are general editors for the series.
Dr. Leary is Professor of English
at California State College at Los Angeles.
He is author of* Thought and Statement *as well as
other texts for high school and college.*

CONSULTANT

*Delores Minor is Supervisor of
High School English in the Detroit Public Schools.*

EDGAR H. KNAPP

RALPH J. WADSWORTH

Student Guide to
IDEAS and
PATTERNS
in Literature III

GENERAL EDITORS:

Edgar H. Knapp

William G. Leary

CONSULTANT: *Delores Minor*

Harcourt Brace Jovanovich, Inc.

New York   Chicago   San Francisco   Atlanta   Dallas

Copyright © 1970 by Harcourt Brace Jovanovich, Inc.

All rights reserved. No part of this publication may be reproduced or transmitted in any form or by any means, electronic or mechanical, including photocopy, recording, or any information storage and retrieval system, without permission in writing from the publisher.

Printed in the United States of America.

ISBN 0–15–339350–5

ACKNOWLEDGMENTS: *For permission to reprint copyrighted material, grateful acknowledgment is made to the following sources:*

AMHERST COLLEGE: Excerpt from "The Private World" by Archibald MacLeish from *Emily Dickinson: Three Views.*

MALCOLM COWLEY: Excerpt from "The Case Against Mr. Frost" by Malcolm Cowley from *New Republic,* copyright 1944 by Editorial Publications.

THE DIAL PRESS, INC.: From "Dear Reader . . . " from *A Bowl of Bishop* by Morris Bishop, copyright © 1954 by Morris Bishop.

E. P. DUTTON & COMPANY, INC.: From Chapter II from the book *The Ordeal of Mark Twain* by Van Wyck Brooks, copyright, 1920, by E. P. Dutton & Co., Inc.; renewal, 1948, by Van Wyck Brooks. From "Our Poets" from the book *Three Essays on America* by Van Wyck Brooks, copyright, 1915, 1934 by E. P. Dutton & Co., Inc.; renewal, 1952, by Van Wyck Brooks.

HARPER & ROW, PUBLISHERS, INCORPORATED: From "Some Remarks on Humor" from *The Second Tree From the Corner* by E. B. White, copyright, 1954 by E. B. White. Excerpt from "How to Tell a Story" in Vol. XXIV, *The Writings of Mark Twain* by Samuel L. Clemens (Harper & Row).

HOLT, RINEHART AND WINSTON, INC.: Excerpt from "Hemingway: The Origins and Meaning of a Style" from *Ernest Hemingway* by Philip Young. Excerpt from *Fire and Ice: The Art and Thought of Robert Frost* by Lawrence Thompson, copyright 1942 by Holt, Rinehart and Winston, Inc. Excerpt from "Walt Whitman" by Mark Van Doren from *There Were Giants in the Land,* copyright 1942, © 1970 by Holt, Rinehart and Winston, Inc.

HOUGHTON MIFFLIN COMPANY: Excerpt from *Passage to Walden* by Reginald L. Cook.

ALFRED A. KNOPF, INC.: Excerpt from "To the Laodiceans" from *Poetry and the Age* by Randall Jarrell. Excerpt from *Letters of Wallace Stevens,* edited by Holly Stevens.

THE MACMILLAN COMPANY: Excerpt from *The Cycle of American Literature* by Robert E. Spiller, The Macmillan Company, 1960. Excerpt from *Literary History of the United States, Third Edition: Revised,* edited by Robert E. Spiller, et al., copyright © 1946, 1947, 1948, 1953, 1963 by The Macmillan Company. Excerpt from *Dark Symphony, Negro Literature in America,* edited by James A. Emmanuel and Theodore L. Gross, copyright © 1968 by The Free Press, A Division of The Macmillan Company.

THE MICHIGAN STATE UNIVERSITY PRESS: Excerpt from "Faulkner: An Introduction, Part Two — The Nobel Prize and the Achievement of Status" from *William Faulkner: Three Decades of Criticism* by Frederick J. Hoffman and Olga W. Vickery, Michigan State University Press, 1960.

WILLIAM MORROW AND COMPANY, INC.: Excerpt from "One's Self I Sing" from *Walt Whitman Reconsidered* by Richard Chase, copyright © 1955 by Richard Chase. Published by William Sloane Associates.

THE NEW AMERICAN LIBRARY, INC.: From Introduction by Alfred Kazin to *U.S.A.* by John Dos Passos, copyright ©, 1969 by The New American Library, Inc., New York.

NEW DIRECTIONS PUBLISHING CORPORATION: Excerpts from "Introduction" by Randall Jarrell from *William Carlos Williams, Selected Poems*, copyright 1949 by William Carlos Williams. From "January Morning," XV by William Carlos Williams from *Collected Earlier Poems*, copyright 1938 by William Carlos Williams.

NEW YORK POST: Excerpt from "Random Notes on This and That" by Richard Watts, Jr., from the *New York Post*, December 2, 1969, © 1969, New York Post Corporation.

THE NEW YORK TIMES: Excerpt from "City Children Find 'Our Town' Alien" from *The New York Times*, August 14, 1969, © 1969 by The New York Times Company. Excerpt from a review of *Selected Poems* by Gwendolyn Brooks from *The New York Times Book Review*, October 6, 1963, © 1963 by The New York Times Company

W. W. NORTON & COMPANY, INC.: Excerpt from *The American Tradition in Literature*, Volume II (Revised) by Scully Bradley, Richard C. Beatty, and E. Hudson Long.

OHIO STATE UNIVERSITY PRESS, LARZER ZIFF, and ROY HARVEY PEARCE: Excerpt from "The Artist and Puritanism" by Larzer Ziff, originally published in *Hawthorne Centenary Essays*, edited by Roy Harvey Pearce, copyright © 1964 by the Ohio State University Press. All rights reserved.

PRINCETON UNIVERSITY PRESS: "The Song of Ch'ang-Kan" from *Ezra Pound's Cathay* by Wai-lim Yip, copyright © 1969 by Princeton University Press.

RANDOM HOUSE, INC.: Excerpt from *Dictionary of Contemporary American Usage*, by Bergen and Cornelia Evans, 1957. Excerpt from "Judgment of the Birds" from *The Immense Journey*, by Loren Eiseley, 1955.

THE SATURDAY EVENING POST COMPANY: Excerpt from review of "The Bride Comes to Yellow Sky" by Al Hine from *Holiday*, March 1953.

SIMON & SCHUSTER, INC.: Excerpt from "Emily Dickinson" from *Makers of the Modern World* by Louis Untermeyer, copyright © 1955 by Louis Untermeyer.

STANFORD UNIVERSITY PRESS: Excerpt from Introduction from *The Fields Were Green* by George Arms (Stanford: Stanford University Press, 1953).

THE REGENTS OF THE UNIVERSITY OF CALIFORNIA: Excerpt from "Willa Cather" from *Spokesman* by T. K. Whipple, published by the University of California Press.

THE UNIVERSITY PRESS OF VIRGINIA: Excerpt from *Faulkner in the University*, Vintage Edition, University of Virginia Press, 1959.

UNIVERSITY PRESS OF WASHINGTON, D.C.: Excerpts from *The America of Carl Sandburg* by Hazel Durnell.

THE VIKING PRESS, INC.: Excerpt from Introduction by Bernard DeVoto from *The Portable Mark Twain*, edited by Bernard DeVoto, copyright 1946 by The Viking Press, Inc.

Contents

Introduction: To the Student

This *Student Guide* is a companion to IDEAS AND PATTERNS IN LITERATURE III. It is intended to help you enjoy the literature in the anthology better by giving you additional information about the writers and by supplying comments and questions that shed light on the literature. The **Study Guide** and **Interaction** questions are not meant as puzzles to be solved or as hurdles to be leaped. Rather, they are — as the title of this book implies — a *guide* to the literature. They point out things you may have missed as you read — for no reader sees the whole of a work of literature in one reading. They are designed to make you see *for yourself* some of the ideas and patterns in these stories, poems, plays, and essays.

The writers included in the anthology created their works for many different reasons. But in every case they wanted to *communicate* something to their readers. They had something to say that was important to themselves and important to mankind; at least they thought so, or they would not have written. They wanted to share their vision, their values, their imagined worlds, with others. To share these things, both the writer and the reader must be willing to submit to "pressure." It is precisely this kind of pressure that yields the rewards of skillful writing and skillful reading. Surely the American poet William Carlos Williams spoke for all writers when he said, in his poem "January Morning,"

> I wanted to write a poem
> that you would understand.
> For what good is it to me
> if you can't understand it?
>   But you got to try hard —

THE ANTHOLOGY

The *Student Guide* follows the organization of the anthology and gives page references to it where helpful. First, then, take a look at IDEAS AND PATTERNS IN LITERATURE III to be sure that you understand its organization and purpose.

IDEAS AND PATTERNS III is divided into four books, each of which begins with works by a well-known American author: Mark Twain, Nathaniel Hawthorne, Stephen Crane, and Thornton Wilder. Each of these opening sections is followed by two or more parts which develop some of the ideas and patterns found in American literature. The selections from Mark Twain which open Book One help illustrate this organization:

1. The Meaning of the Frontier
   (As one of the earliest and best reporters of the Mississippi and far western frontiers, Twain helped form the myth of the frontier in the American imagination.)

2. American Humor
   (Twain discovered that American humor was a unique art, and he became its leading practitioner, both on stage and in print.)

3. The American Language
   (Twain was the first great American writer to use native American speech as the basis for his prose.)

COMMENTS

From time to time you will find comments on the selection or author you are studying. These **Comments** are not meant to hand you "truths" to be accepted without thinking. They are intended to stimulate your own thinking and to point out some possible interpretations which may not have occurred to you. The **Comments** give you an opportunity to see the way other readers have reacted to what you are reading.

THE STUDY GUIDES

The questions under the heading **Study Guide** are of many kinds. They are meant to be just what their heading says: a *guide to* closer and more careful reading of the literature. Most of the questions are inductive; that is, they ask you to think for yourself, to "draw out" the answers through reasoning. Often these questions are worded in such a way that they point you in the direction of an answer. Sometimes they contain additional comments by the editors or helpful background information.

The **Interaction** questions are more far-ranging than the ones in the **Study Guide.** The **Study Guide** questions ask you to think only about what the author has put down on the page. The **Interaction** questions go beyond this. They assume that you have read and understood the selection. They use the literature as a kind of springboard for a wider discussion of the ideas and patterns of literature. Often they ask you to look for the connections between two or more works.

The **Interaction** questions, as a rule, do not have one "right" answer. They ask for your opinion — but always an opinion backed up by evidence in the literature itself.

Edgar H. Knapp
William G. Leary
GENERAL EDITORS

Book One | Part 1

MARK TWAIN

No writer is more central to American literature than Mark Twain, perhaps because the locale of his best work — the Mississippi valley and the West — is so clearly the land of a new people, a new nation. Twain was our first great writer to grow up west of the Mississippi. There had been, of course, other great American writers before him, such as Hawthorne, Thoreau, and Emerson. But to both Americans and Europeans of his time, no writer had so uniquely an American voice as this self-educated humorist from the frontier.

Like "The Story of the Old Ram," "The Pony Express," and "The Quarles Farm," the chapters from *Old Times on the Mississippi* tell about a time in American life that had already vanished before Twain wrote about it. A kind of heroic, legendary stature is given to the stately ships, to their pilots, and to the river itself. In this book Mark Twain not only captured a part of the American past, but the passions and dreams of his own youth as well.

Mark Twain wrote his autobiography over and over again. His greatest works retell and embellish his own life's adventures. In a sense Twain turned his life into a tall tale. It is as much a part of American literature as *Huckleberry Finn* and *Tom Sawyer*.

Born Samuel Langhorne Clemens on November 30, 1835, Twain grew up in Hannibal, Missouri. This frontier town, Twain later wrote, was "a heavenly place for a boy." There he dreamed of being a pirate, smoked foul cigars behind his house, was terrorized by the real Injun Joe, and saw firsthand the evils of slavery. He met Tom Blankenship, the original Huck Finn. And he began a lifelong love affair with the Mississippi River. The rich adventures of his youth provided Twain with endless materials for writing.

When his father died, the eleven-year-old Twain left school to become a printer's apprentice. For the next fifteen years he worked at various jobs — as a printer, reporter, and riverboat pilot. During this period Twain began rehearsing for his literary career by writing humorous newspaper sketches. Twain embellished the story of his

1

early writing, as he did so many events in his life, by attributing his "scribbling itch" to a sudden inspiration: walking along the streets of Hannibal one day (Twain wrote) he happened on a page from a book about Joan of Arc. The story of the French martyr was to have great significance to him all his life. It taught him the "magic of the printed word."

After a short term of service in the Confederate Army, Twain joined his brother Orion out West during the height of the Gold Rush. Unsuccessful at prospecting, Twain went to work as a reporter for the Virginia City *Territorial Enterprise*. Combining facts about the frontier with broad humor, Twain's stories gave him a reputation as a "phunny phellow." In 1866 he met Artemus Ward, the most popular humorous lecturer of the day. Twain tried his own hand as a literary comedian, imitating Ward. In his public performances he would impersonate characters he had met or invented. The result was that he developed a keen ear for American dialect, both as a writer and a lecturer.

In 1867 Twain persuaded a San Francisco newspaper to send him abroad as a correspondent. For the next few years he traveled, wrote, and led a carefree life. Then he traveled East to become editor of the Buffalo *Express* and to marry Olivia Langdon, whom he had met on his travels. Having learned the value of the spoken language as a lecturer, Twain tested *Roughing It* and *Innocents Abroad* by reading them aloud to his wife.

These two humorous travel books, based on his experiences in the West and in Europe, made Twain famous as a spinner of entertaining yarns. Their success encouraged Twain to give up editing in order to concentrate on writing and lecturing. "My sole idea," he wrote of this period in his life, "was to make comic capital out of everything I saw or heard." But he soon grew weary of the label "phunny phellow." He wanted his writing to be authentic.

Twain went back to the authentic materials of his boyhood experiences for his next and greatest works — *Tom Sawyer*, *Huckleberry Finn*, and *Old Times on the Mississippi*. He used satire more often, and his colloquial style was praised as a model of realistic writing. In *Huckleberry Finn* and later in *Pudd'nhead Wilson* he delved more deeply than he had before into moral dilemmas. These two books show him as an early champion of rights for Negroes. His picture of the escaped slave, Jim, in *Huckleberry Finn* is one of the most dignified and sympathetic portraits in American literature. But Twain's readers persisted in seeing him only as a comedian.

Literary success and family coziness at Hartford, Connecticut, made the late 1870's and 1880's a period of great happiness for Twain. He adored his wife and three daughters and enjoyed his success as an author, lecturer, and publisher. But beginning in 1894, a series of shocks produced another Mark Twain, the bitter satirist who wrote:

Whoever has lived long enough to find out what life is, knows how deep a debt of gratitude we owe to Adam, the first great benefactor of our race. He brought death into the world.

Although Twain scorned the money hunger that possessed Americans after the Civil War, he fell victim to that very hunger. He invested his money in a typesetting machine and ended in bankruptcy. His disgust with his own greed and his unconquerable longing to be rich darkened his outlook on the human race. To repay all his creditors, he embarked on an exhaustive lecture tour. Before he had repaid all his debts, his daughter Susy died. Within the next eight years Twain also lost his wife, Livy, and his daughter Jean. Twain was left a lonely and embittered man.

The disillusionment of his last years Twain poured into his writing; his humor became sharp irony. "The Man That Corrupted Hadleyburg" and *The Mysterious Stranger* are from this period. They express Twain's conviction of the selfishness of the human race.

By the turn of the century Twain was an internationally celebrated humorist. Notable people — such as Helen Keller and Rudyard Kipling — flocked to visit and interview him. The public applauded his lectures. Universities here and abroad awarded him honors and degrees. And after his death in 1910 Twain became even more celebrated. A new generation of writers saw him as more than a humorist. Ernest Hemingway, for example, saw Twain as an innovator in bringing the spoken language of the times into literature, which led him to say, "All modern American literature comes from one book by Mark Twain called *Huckleberry Finn*."

Comment

. . . Mark's principal service to the American language was not Huck's vernacular: it lay within the recognized limits of literary prose. Within those limits he was a radical innovator, a prime mover who changed the medium by incorporating in it the syntax, the idioms, and especially the vocabulary of the common life. The vigor of his prose comes directly from the speech of the Great Valley and the Far West. A superlative may be ventured: Mark Twain had a greater effect than any other writer on the evolution of American prose. . . .

Any unidentified quotation from Mark Twain will be recognized at sight as American. It is, furthermore, a national Americanism; his great books are set along the Mississippi, but no one can think of them as local or regional. But there is also a kind of centripetal Americanism, so that he seems frequently to speak for the nation.

— BERNARD DE VOTO: The Portable Mark Twain

The Story of the Old Ram

Text pages 3–7

Mark Twain described Jim Blaine's wandering tale this way:

The idea of the tale is to exhibit certain bad effects of a good memory: the sort of memory which is too good, which remembers everything and forgets nothing, which has no sense of proportion and can't tell an important event from an unimportant one but preserves them all, states them all, and thus retards the progress of a narrative, at the same time making a tangled, inextricable confusion of it, intolerably wearisome to the listener. The historian of "The Story of the Old Ram" had that kind of a memory. He often tried to communicate that history to his comrades, and other surface miners, but he could never complete it because his memory defeated his every attempt to march a straight course; it persistently threw remembered details in his way that had nothing to do with the tale; these unrelated details would interest him and sidetrack him; if he came across a name or a family or any other thing that had nothing to do with his tale he could diverge from his course to tell about the person who owned that name or explain all about that family — with the result that as he plodded on he always got further and further from his grandfather's memorable adventure with the ram, and finally went to sleep before he got to the end of the story, and so did his comrades. Once he did manage to approach so nearly to the end, apparently, that the boys were filled with an eager hope; they believed that at last they were going to find out all about the grandfather's adventure and what it was that had happened.

Although Jim's story is a wandering tale, the incidents that sidetrack him all have one thing in common: each is grotesque and outlandish. The story should be read aloud if you want to get the full flavor of it. If possible, listen to the reading by Hal Holbrook on *Mark Twain Tonight!* (Columbia Records).

Study Guide

1. **Humor.** This story represents Twain the humorist. Both humor and comedy are hard to define, and it has often been said that a joke is spoiled as soon as someone starts to analyze it. In your opinion what is the *main point* of the humor in this tale? What are some other aspects of it that make it humorous?

2. In "How to Tell a Story" Twain discusses the art of American humor.

> There are several kinds of stories, but only one difficult kind — the humorous. I will talk mainly about that one. The humorous story is American, the comic story is English, the witty story is French. The humorous story depends for its effect upon the *manner* of the telling; the comic and the witty story upon the *matter*.
>
> The humorous story may be spun out to great length, and may wander around as much as it pleases, and arrive nowhere in particular; but the comic and witty stories must be brief and end with a point. The humorous story bubbles gently along, the others burst.
>
> The humorous story is strictly a work of art — high and delicate art — and only an artist can tell it; but no art is necessary in telling the comic and the witty story; anybody can do it. The art of telling a humorous story — understand, I mean by word of mouth, not print — was created in America, and has remained at home.
>
> The humorous story is told gravely; the teller does his best to conceal the fact that he even dimly suspects that there is anything funny about it; but the teller of the comic story tells you beforehand that it is one of the funniest things he has ever heard, then tells it with eager delight, and is the first person to laugh when he gets through. And sometimes, if he has had good success, he is so glad and happy that he will repeat the "nub" of it and glance around from face to face, collecting applause, and then repeat it again. It is a pathetic thing to see.
>
> To string incongruities and absurdities together in a wandering and sometimes purposeless way, and seem innocently unaware that they are absurdities, is the basis of the American art, if my position is correct. Another feature is the slurring of the point. A third is the dropping of a studied remark apparently without knowing it, as if one were thinking aloud. The fourth and last is the pause.

   a) Pick out from "The Story of the Old Ram" two examples of incongruities and absurdities strung together "in a wandering and sometimes purposeless way."

   b) What do you think Twain meant by "the slurring of the point"? Can you find examples?

   c) What remarks in the story seem to correspond to the third feature of the humorous story — "the dropping of a studied remark apparently without knowing it"?

d) "The fourth and last is the pause." Pick out two places in the story where control of the pause is absolutely essential to the success of the story.

The Pony Express

Text pages 8–10

Comment

The West, when it began to put itself into literature, could do so without the sense, or the apparent sense, of any older or politer world outside of it; whereas the East was always looking fearfully over its shoulder at Europe, and anxious to account for itself as well as represent itself. No such anxiety as this entered Mark Twain's mind, and it is not claiming too much for the Western influence upon American literature to say that the final liberation of the East from this anxiety is due to the West, and to its ignorant courage or its indifference to its difference from the rest of the world. . . .

The Western boy of forty or fifty years ago grew up so close to the primeval woods or fields that their inarticulate poetry became part of his being, and he was apt to deal simply and uncritically with literature when he turned to it, as he dealt with nature. He took what he wanted, and left what he did not like; he used it for the playground, not the workshop of his spirit. Something like this I find true of Mark Twain in peculiar and uncommon measure.

— WILLIAM DEAN HOWELLS

Study Guide

1. The headnote in the text (page 8) suggests that there is a "legend-making" process at work in Twain's account of the Pony Express rider. In other words, this is not strictly a piece of objective reporting. Find some phrases from the essay that show that Mark Twain was impressed by the romantic legend of the Pony Express rider and wanted to convey his feelings to the reader. What are some words or phrases that would be out of place in a strictly objective piece of reporting?
2. **Punctuation for expression.** As in "The Story of the Old Ram," you can hear a definite American "speaking voice" telling this story. In this case, however, the voice is not that of a character

such as Jim Blaine, but of Twain himself. Notice how he uses punctuation as an expressive device, especially the many exclamation points and the italic type. What emotion does he emphasize through these marks of punctuation?

3. Twain turns the hard-working rider into a magical figure by using images, metaphors, and similes. Be ready to rewrite each of the following phrases showing how a more literal-minded writer might have expressed the thought:
   a) He rode fifty miles without stopping, by daylight, moonlight, starlight, or through the blackness of darkness. . . . (page 8)
   b) He wore a little wafer of a racing saddle. . . . (page 9)
   c) . . . these were written on paper as airy and thin as gold leaf, nearly. . . . (page 9)
   d) . . . man and horse burst past our excited faces and go swinging away like a belated fragment of a storm! (page 10)

4. In the last paragraph, what is the significance of the "flake of white foam left quivering and perishing on a mail sack"? What else is perishing besides the flake of foam itself?

The Quarles Farm

Text pages 11–13

Study Guide

1. In discussing "The Pony Express" we saw that Twain was not writing a strictly objective report. He was telling his readers about something he remembered — and telling it so sharply that the reader could share the experience — but he was also giving the reader his own feelings and attitudes toward the event. "The Quarles Farm," too, is not a cold, objective report. It is obvious that this place represented to Twain a place of joy, peace, innocence, and wonder. Where in this piece do you see a "myth-making" or "legend-making" process at work?

2. This essay is notable for its fine detail. As a matter of fact, there is little story or narrative to it. By accumulating details, Twain builds up a sense of time and place. A less imaginative writer might have let it go at this: "When I was a boy I spent many happy months at the Quarles Farm." Twain *gives* you the farm itself — at least a strong impression of it. Because he is an old

man looking back over many years, there is a great intensity to the opening words: *I can see the farm yet.* . . . Discuss Twain's handling of detail in this selection. What are some of the details that seem to you particularly vivid, particularly well expressed?

3. How does Twain use nature as a symbol in this selection? Look especially at the last paragraph.

Interaction

1. In contrast to life in modern America, life on a farm like the Quarles farm would be considered harsh. None of the "conveniences" we take for granted were available. Is there any suggestion in this selection that life on this frontier farm was difficult or lonely? What have those of us who live in towns and cities lost and gained compared to those who lived on the Quarles farm as Twain portrays it?

2. Compare this selection with "The Pony Express" with regard to the voice of the speaker. What differences in tone, mood, and rhythm do you detect?

from Old Times on the Mississippi

Text pages 14–31

Comment

It was not a sentimental regret . . . that lifelong hankering for the lost paradise of the pilothouse. It was something more organic, and Mark Twain provides us with an explanation. "If I have seemed to love my subject," he says, among the impassioned pages of his book, "it is no surprising thing, for I loved the profession far better than any I have followed since, and I took a measureless pride in it." A singular statement for a man to make out of the fullness of a literary life, the two pillars of which, if it has any pillars, are surely nothing else than love and pride! But Mark Twain writes those words with an almost unctuous gravity of conviction, and this, in so many words, is what he says: as a pilot he had experienced the full flow of the creative life as he had not experienced it in literature. . . . The life of a Mississippi pilot had, in some special way, satisfied the instinct of the artist in him; in quite this way, the instinct of the artist had never been satisfied again.

— Van Wyck Brooks: The Ordeal of Mark Twain

Study Guide

CHAPTERS 1–2

1. The opening chapter forms a prologue to the whole of *Old Times*. The first two sentences present the topic which is to be developed. Then the river, the steamboats, the life of a pilot are set forth as seen through the eyes of a boy. How does Twain give each of the following a glamorous, legendary stature?
   a) the Mississippi
   b) the arriving steamboat
   c) the pilot's life

2. **Tone.** "When I was a boy," the opening words, clearly and immediately indicate that the narrator is an adult looking back on some of the incidents of his life. This narrator, the "speaking voice" of the work, not only tells the reader what happened but also how he, the writer, felt about the events then and how he feels about them now. Take, for example, this sentence: "Now and then we had a hope that, if we lived and were good, God would permit us to be pirates." In these few words Twain suggests that aura of excitement, the innocence, the seriousness, and the mischievousness that characterized his boyhood; he lets us see how intense he was.

   When we speak of *tone*, we mean this speaking voice of the narrator and the distance between him and his subject matter. *Tone* can be defined as the author's attitude toward his subject. It is complicated here because the author is two people: the young apprentice and the older narrator. Through *Old Times* the reader sees the action with a kind of double vision.

   How is the incident of the night watchman (pages 20–21) an example of this double vision? What was the attitude of the author as a young boy toward steamboatmen and life on the river? What is Twain's attitude now toward himself as a young boy?

CHAPTER 3

1. This chapter introduces Mr. Bixby, who, next to Twain himself, is the leading character in *Old Times*. When Mr. Bixby agreed to teach Twain the Mississippi, Twain "supposed that all a pilot had to do was to keep his boat in the river, and . . . did not consider that that could be much of a trick." What changes his mind?

2. What makes Twain realize that "piloting was not quite so romantic as I had imagined it was"? (page 24) What had he expected it to be like?

3. What makes Twain say, ". . . the romance and beauty were all gone from the river"? (page 26) Does the older Twain, the narrator, share this attitude? Twain says that he wonders sometimes whether a man "has gained most or lost most by learning his trade." What did Twain gain? What did he lose?

CHAPTER 4

1. What skills does Bixby teach Twain? How does he try to build Twain's character? How does he instill in Twain a sense of humility?

2. Mr. Bixby gives Twain a test. What was Bixby testing? What method did he use? What did Twain learn from this test? How did Twain feel when he found he had been tricked? What is the narrator's attitude toward the trick? What was your reaction to it?

3. Characterization. An author who wants his readers to see his characters clearly has the job of showing these characters in situations which reveal their traits. He cannot say, "Mr. Bixby was kind," and expect all his readers to accept that. If, however, he *shows* Mr. Bixby doing some kind deed, or saying something with kindness, not just once but enough times to set up a pattern of kindness, then the alert reader reaches the logical conclusion. This act on the part of the reader is called making *inferences*. In the character of Mr. Bixby, Twain sets up such a pattern; he selects the events which show what Mr. Bixby is like without actually telling us. The character of Mr. Bixby is brought home to the reader mainly by implication.

What are Mr. Bixby's outsanding character traits? How does Twain show that Mr. Bixby was a skillful and proud pilot?

CHAPTER 5

Twain uses both comparison and contrast to support his statement that "a pilot, in those days, was the only unfettered and entirely independent human being that lived in the earth." (page 30) What comparisons and contrasts does he use to develop this idea? In what ways was the pilot "entirely independent"? What restrictions and disciplines did his work demand?

Interaction

1. Compare the account of the arrival of the steamboat (pages 15–16) with Twain's account of the Pony Express rider. What similarities in attitude do you find? In the preceding **Study Guide,** you have considered Twain's use of language. Find some examples in the first two paragraphs of *Old Times* (pages 14–15) of language that is vivid and conveys excitement.

2. The critic Van Wyck Brooks complained that Twain glamorized the frontier. "How many books have been published of late years letting us behind the scenes of the glamorous myth of pioneering!" he wrote. What aspects of piloting were "glamorous" to the young Twain? to the adult Twain? Do you think "glamorous" is the best word to describe piloting as Twain sees it? Explain your answer. What romantic attitudes does the older Twain have toward each of the following?
   - a) the Mississippi
   - b) the science of piloting
   - c) the life of the pilot

   Does he give us an indication of the unromantic and dangerous side of each?

3. Are there any trades or professions in our own day that allow someone to be as "unfettered and entirely independent" as the riverboat pilot? If so, what are they? Are there any that are as romantic and adventurous as piloting a riverboat? What do you think they are? How would a young person have to go about learning these kinds of work? How does Twain's method of learning the science of piloting differ from the modern methods of learning a trade or profession?

4. One of the most persistent patterns in American literature is that of the quest or search. The hero is often like the knight in medieval literature who set out in search of the Holy Grail or some other symbol of the ideal. What is the young Mark Twain searching for in *Old Times*? What is the storyteller, the older Mark Twain, searching for?

Mark Twain: Summing Up

1. Many of the notions we have about the frontier have been fostered by movies, television, and authors like Twain. What aspects of frontier life does Twain picture in these selections? How does this picture differ from the typical western?

2. **Style.** Many modern American writers acknowledge a debt to Mark Twain, for, as T. S. Eliot wrote, he "discovered a new way of writing" by creating "a literary language based on American colloquial speech." William Dean Howells, a critic of Twain's day who sometimes edited his works, also remarked on Twain's natural style:

> . . . So far as I know, Mr. Clemens is the first writer to use in extended writing the fashion we all use in thinking, and to set down the thing that comes into his mind without fear or favor of the thing that went before or the thing that may be about to follow. I, for instance, in putting this paper together, am anxious to observe some sort of logical order, to discipline such impressions and notions as I have of the subject into a coherent body which shall march so columnwise to a conclusion obvious if not inevitable from the start. But Mr. Clemens, if he were writing it, would not be anxious to do any such thing.

One example of Twain's colloquial style is, "But that did the business for me. My imagination began to construct dangers out of nothing, and they multipled faster than I could keep the run of them." (page 29) What other examples of colloquial style (not including the dialogue) do you find in *Old Times?*

3. Some great American writers are not particularly popular. That is, few of us pick them up to read just for pleasure. But Twain has always been a widely read author. What do you think there is in his subject and style that makes him so popular with readers?

THE MEANING OF THE FRONTIER

Note that the title of this section is not "The Frontier" but "The *Meaning* of the Frontier." In other words, it is not concerned with the American frontier as it actually was (which is the business of historians) but rather with what the frontier *became* for Americans, the legend that sprang from the reality. The questions and comments in the following pages emphasize this "myth-making" or "legend-making" process of literature as it applies to the frontier. It is generally agreed that the West is "the homeland of the essential American myth," that the frontier became a symbol which greatly helped shape the American mind: it suggested the freedom of an unstructured society in which every man could shake off the past and begin life anew. It suggested an individualism which at best was heroic, at worst lawless. There was an epic quality to the conquest and settlement of the West, and the memory of it instills pride in Americans.

John Colter's Race for Life

Text pages 36–43

Stanley Vestal   *born:* 1887

Stanley Vestal is the penname of Walter Stanley Campbell. For many years a teacher of writing at the University of Oklahoma, Professor Campbell has become known as an authority on the old Southwest and on the Indians of Oklahoma and New Mexico. His family history and his friendship with the Cheyennes have resulted in many novels and histories about the Old West. One critic wrote of Vestal that he holds fast to the facts "without even a side glance at Hollywood." Some of his books are *Kit Carson*, *Mountain Men*, and *New Sources of Indian History*.

Study Guide

1. One reason why the story is engrossing and exciting is that Vestal makes it come to life. How does he make the reader feel that he

is observing the story at close range rather than from a distance?

2. Why was Colter sent into the lands of the Blackfeet?

3. **Point of view.** What picture of the Indians — Crows and Black-feet — do you find in this account of Colter's adventures? From whose point of view are the Indians seen and judged? Does Vestal explain the Indians' point of view?

4. What dangers and challenges presented in this story have be-came part of the legend of the frontier?

Interaction

In studying Mark Twain's "The Pony Express" you saw how Twain built up a heroic picture of the pony rider by using figurative language and words with favorable connotations. Compare Twain's description with the description in this story about Colter. Does Stanley Vestal use the same kind of language to describe his hero? How does he present Colter as an admirable figure?

Strong Men, Riding Horses

Text page 43

GWENDOLYN BROOKS   *born:* 1917

At the age of seven Gwendolyn Brooks began putting rhymes to-gether. As a high school student she contributed to the Chicago *Defender.* After attending junior college, she continued to write poetry and acknowledges a debt to adult education classes in mod-ern poetry. Her poems, many of which are about life in Chicago's black communities, have won prizes and fellowships, including the Pulitzer Prize in 1950. Gwendolyn Brooks still lives and works in Chicago. Among her works are *Annie Allen, Bronzeville Boys, Se-lected Poems,* and *We Real Cool.*

In this poem Gwendolyn Brooks re-creates the thoughts of a mod-ern western fan — Lester, who cannot help but draw comparisons between the Strong Men of his own day and western heroes, be-tween his urban environment and the cowboys' wide-open spaces, between himself and the pioneers.

Comment

[Miss Brooks] has a warm heart, a cool head, and practices the art of poetry with professional naturalness. Her ability to distinguish between what is sad and what is silly is unfailing, and she deals with race, love, war, and other matters with uncommon common sense and a mellow humor that is as much a rarity as it is a relief.

— The *New York Times* Book Review

Study Guide

1. Beginning with the words "Except that Strong Men are," Lester describes the "heroes" of his own day. What are these Strong Men and their lives like? Does Lester admire them? What words convey his attitude toward them? What is meant by the words "From hope to crying"?
2. How does Lester feel his own character differs from the Strong Men's?
3. What contrast does the poem set up between the frontier days and our own times?

The Outcasts of Poker Flat

Text pages 44–54

BRET HARTE   1836–1902

Francis Bret Harte, at one time hailed as a "new prophet in American letters," was born in Albany, New York. His parents encouraged him to read and travel, and at sixteen he found himself in California as a printer's assistant. His writing career met an early setback when he was fired for exposing a frontiersmen's massacre of an Indian community. But after his poems and his famous "The Luck of Roaring Camp" were published, he was in great demand as a writer and lecturer. He was appointed U.S. commercial agent in Germany, where he continued writing until his death in 1902.

Although Harte's reputation has been debated by critics, he is the acknowledged inaugurator of "the philosophic strain" in western humor. Constance Rourke writes, "Harte created tragi-comedy. For the first time . . . elements of the humor of defeat appeared" in stories of the frontier.

Comment

Harte was no prude; he drew no morals and preached no sermons; he painted prostitutes and foul-mouthed children and drunken sots without apology. . . . He had humor, a good ear, a style that was disciplined and clean. Yet through all, even his best work, runs a thread of something theatrical and false.

— WALLACE STEGNER in Literary History of the United States

Study Guide

1. **Tone.** What picture of frontier justice does Harte portray in the opening paragraphs? What is his tone or attitude toward this kind of justice? Does he approve or disapprove? Or does he suspend personal judgment? Explain with references to the story.
2. **Local color.** What are some of the picturesque "western" details in this story which made it so popular with readers "back East"? Consider the choice of characters, the language, the settings, and the customs described.
3. **Sentimentality.** In a sentimental story emotion is exaggerated and overstated. Details are supplied to make the reader react emotionally to an extent not fully justified by the situation. Do you think this is a sentimental story? Consider the following incidents:
    a) Oakhurst's refusal to save himself by going on alone.
    b) Oakhurst's giving back the money he has won from Tommy.
    c) The innocence of the young lovers.
    d) The outcasts' singing a hymn in the snow.
    e) The death of Mother Shipton.
    f) The softened heart of the rough Duchess.
    g) Oakhurst's final sacrifice and his epitaph.
4. How were the outcasts unfit for life on the frontier?
5. Explain the statement that Oakhurst was "at once the strongest and yet the weakest of the outcasts of Poker Flat."
6. In your own words, state the theme of this story as you understand it. The theme will necessarily be a general statement. Remember that such a statement is not a substitute for the story itself and that it cannot contain the full meaning of the story. Be careful to avoid a statement so general that it describes almost any story. For example, *Frontier life was full of danger* is obviously too general for "The Outcasts of Poker Flat." On the other hand a statement such as *Gamblers are capable of kindness and generosity* is too narrow.

Interaction

Wallace Stegner, a modern writer of the Canadian and American frontier, says of frontier writers: "There were in general two kinds of people who wrote this literature: those who knew what they were talking about, and those who did not; those who aimed to tell the truth, and those who did not." Discuss this statement in relation to "The Pony Express," "John Colter's Race for Life," and "The Outcasts of Poker Flat." Does each of the writers seem to know what he is talking about? Which of them "dresses up" his experience? Is this "dressing up" necessarily dishonest?

The Role of the Undesirables

Text pages 55–64

ERIC HOFFER   *born:* 1902

Eric Hoffer is a self-educated San Francisco longshoreman. Before becoming a philosopher and writer, he was a manual laborer for forty years, working as an itinerant farm hand, dishwasher, lumberjack, construction worker, and prospector. Wherever he worked he took his books and his library card; in the fields and workyards during breaks he wrote of the men and movements he observed. In 1968 President Lyndon Johnson appointed Hoffer to the Commission to Study Violence.

Comment

Basic to Hoffer's thought is the conviction that "the only new thing in history is America . . ." where "the common people could do things."   — KENNETH CRAWFORD in *Newsweek*

The word *essay* originally meant a "trial" or "attempt" to say something meaningful about a subject. Most essays are attempts to convince the reader that the author's ideas, arguments, or visions are true and should be adopted. Persuasive writing must be read with care, however. Many writers, in their eagerness to convince you, confuse statements of fact (which can be proved true or false) with statements of opinion (which cannot be proved either true or false). The reader of an essay must be alert to this confusion. He may not be able to find immediate evidence proving the truth or falsity of a statement of fact. But he can judge statements of opinion and find them reasonable or not, according to the author's skill in supporting his opinion.

Study Guide

1. In the light of the essay as a whole, is the author's statement that "this country was built, largely, by hordes of undesirables" a statement of fact or a statement of opinion? Can its truth or falseness be tested in any way? Do you accept Hoffer's definition of *undesirable?* To what extent does the validity of his statement depend on his definition of *undesirable?*

2. Does it make any difference to the quality of Hoffer's essay if you decide that his thesis is a statement of fact or a statement of opinion? Explain.

3. *Undesirables* is a charged word. Does the title mean the same thing to you when you have finished the essay as it did when you started it? How has the author defined the term? Has he drawn a surprising conclusion from his definition?

4. What is the purpose of the personal narrative at the beginning of the essay? What does it tell about the author and his point of view? What part does his personal experience play in his argument?

5. Which of the following statements most accurately describes this essay? Discuss each of the three statements and show why it is, or is not, a good criticism of the essay:

    a) Hoffer has drawn up his arguments and facts carefully and presented them in an orderly way. A careful reader will be forced to agree with him about who the pioneers were.

    b) In 1934 Hoffer had a personal experience which gave him an insight about American pioneers. He draws a careful analogy between his vision of modern migrants and those who settled the country. Based on this analogy and on our general knowledge of human nature we may find his argument illuminating and agree that he is probably right.

    c) Hoffer himself has been a tramp and migrant worker. He appears to wish to elevate and romanticize the lowest elements of society. His argument is not convincing because it is pure speculation.

Interaction

1. In what way does Hoffer's idea (that the West was largely settled by "undesirables") apply to the following characters in the earlier selections in this section?
   a) John Oakhurst ("Outcasts of Poker Flat")
   b) Tommy and Piney ("Outcasts of Poker Flat")
   c) John Colter
2. **Generalizations.** It would be difficult for us to communicate with each other without making generalized statements. But in considering the truth in a generalization you must consider its limitations, its exceptions, and its content. Look at the following generalization from Hoffer's essay. (page 59) To what extent do you think it true?

   A man rarely leaves a soft spot and goes deliberately in search of hardship and privation. . . . A man who has made good and has a standing in his community stays put.
3. Discuss the following quotation from Hoffer's essay and its implications for your own community and for America today: "There is in us a tendency to judge a race, a nation, or an organization by its least worthy members." (page 62)

   You may agree or disagree or take a position midway between agreement and disagreement. Support your discussion with reference to personal experiences, current events, or history. Since Hoffer has listed three things which we have a tendency to judge (a race, a nation, an organization), a good way to structure your argument might be (a) to begin and end with a general statement of your position, and (b) to support your ideas with three paragraphs taking up each of these items in turn.

Texas Massacre

Text pages 65–66

WALT WHITMAN   (biography text pages 356–357)

The violence of our frontier past has virtually transcended historical fact to become legendary. Violence and killing, still very real in our own time, tore Texas apart in the 1830's. The frontiersmen of Texas, isolated from Mexico by geographical, cultural, and language barriers, began to form companies of revolutionaries to fight for independence. On March 6, 1836, the Mexican General Santa Anna destroyed to a man the revolutionaries at the Alamo. Thirteen days later Colonel James W. Fannin's forces were captured, and, on orders from Santa Anna, slaughtered. Though not as well known as the Battle of the Alamo, the Massacre of Goliad is part of the violent history of the Old West.

Study Guide

1. Whitman opens with "Now I tell what I knew in Texas in my early youth." In fact, Whitman was never in Texas. What does this opening add to the poem? *person fond to it*
2. **Diction.** Find words that convey Whitman's attitude toward the rangers. What is his attitude toward their murderers?
3. How does the poem build a sense of the frontier as a stage for heroic action? *He builds up the men from the Alamo as heros that were brave until their death.*

On a Naked Hill in Wyoming

Text pages 66–67

WILSON O. CLOUGH

Wilson O. Clough (rhymes with *now*) was born in New Jersey and makes his home in Laramie, Wyoming. He is a professor at the University of Wyoming and the author of poems, stories, and books on American culture.

Professor Clough is interested in the study questions textbooks have used for "On a Naked Hill in Wyoming." One such question asked, "What does the bird at the end of stanza three represent?" Professor Clough answers, "I've been wondering about the answer myself." In a letter to the editors of this book, Wilson O. Clough talked about his intentions in the poem:

. . . the poem attempted to make use of Wyoming's rather austere scenery, actually northeastern Wyoming, and a deserted coal-mining camp in a deep gorge running westward out of the Black Hills foothills country in Crook County. The Italian legend on the tombstone was actual, and the graveyard on its stark sloping hillside above the gorge looked westward on the silent scenery. . . . The general impression was intended to be that of the big West taking over man's temporary invasions for exploitation, both of land and of people.

Study Guide

1. **Organization.** This poem is organized spatially or scenically, almost like frames shot by a motion picture camera. We first see the abandoned graveyard closeup, focusing on a few of the stones and grave markers; next the dark mountains in the far distance; then the ghost mine and town three miles away; at last we return to a close-up of one of the gravestones. Why does the poem begin and end with the same words? Why is the phrase *O carissima mia, addio* repeated toward the end of the poem?

2. What is the reader to infer from the Greek, Serbian, German, and Italian names on the stones? What has happened to the mining town?

3. We are accustomed to thinking of industry and its ugly offshoots as characteristic of modern times "back East" rather than of the old days in the "wild West." How has the ghost town created an "ugly gash yawning" in the landscape? How is the frontier resuming its original character?

The Bride Comes to Yellow Sky

Text pages 68–103

JAMES AGEE   1909–1955

James Agee grew up in the Cumberland Country in Tennessee. After attending Harvard, where he won awards for his poetry, he worked on the staffs of the news magazines *Fortune, Time,* and *The Nation.* He took time off to live with and learn about the lives of sharecroppers, and drawing on those experiences he wrote *Let Us Now Praise Famous Men.* He then turned to writing for the movies and television and brought to these media such artistically and popularly acclaimed scripts as *The African Queen.*

The Bride Comes to Yellow Sky was paired with the screen adaptation of Joseph Conrad's "The Secret Sharer." Together these films were called *Face to Face* and brought Agee high praise for experimenting successfully with cinematic short stories. When the film was released in 1952, Arthur Knight, a noted film critic, wrote of *The Bride:*

James Agee's slyly humorous script expertly expands Crane's short story for the screen, retaining all his vast affection for western types on a passing frontier. . . .

After his death, James Agee's reputation continued to grow. His novel A *Death in the Family* was made into a successful play and movie. His essays, collected in *Agee on Film*, are now considered outstanding film criticism, and his screenplays are studied as important examples of film art.

Comment

It is a wonderfully sad and funny movie. Minor Watson's Scratchy is the nicest and most believable old bad man you will ever see. There is disturbingly wonderful photography in the scene where Scratchy is getting drunk, where the camera reels and smears with his drunken lurches. Marjorie Steele is perfect as the new bride, both bright and naive when confronted with the splendors of a nineteenth-century dining car, proud of her big sheriff husband and delighted with her trousseau finery. A beautifully realized job which never falls into either stock hick portrayal or overglamorization. [Robert] Preston is lovably stuffy as the sheriff.

— AL HINE: *Review of* The Bride Comes to Yellow Sky

Films are much more akin to fiction than they are to staged drama. Susanne K. Langer, a modern philosopher, points out that at a play your physical point of view is fixed by the location of your seat, but at a movie your eye is the camera's eye and your ear, the microphone's ear. When a play moves forward or back in time — to simulate thoughts or dreams — you are more or less an observer. When a movie does the same thing, you are a participant.

How does a movie achieve these effects? Principally through camera directions. Note that in Agee's script there are two main types of camera directions. The first tells you how the camera moves, what it *sees*, when it cuts from one fact to another, from one scene to another. The second kind of camera direction tells the moviemaker and the actor what to include in their work. All of the meaning of a movie is not in the dialogue the actors speak. One of the most important camera directions in this script comes toward the very end: "Salient are the torn pictures of the murderous faces and weapons of early western fiction." Think about the way in which these visual images contribute to the meaning of the movie as a whole.

Study Guide

1. **Comedy.** This film script dramatizes a turning point in the life of a frontier community in terms of comedy. Look at the first short scene in the movie — between Potter and the Prisoner. How does (Agee) establish right at the start that this story will take place in the world of comedy?
2. **Structure.** Agee has two lines of action which move forward together — Potter and his Bride on the train; and the events that are happening at the same time back in Yellow Sky. The movie switches back and forth between these two settings. The final scenes bring the two lines of action together. What dramatic advantage does the film gain from cutting back and forth?
3. **Character.** Scratchy, "the last of the old gang," is not a very admirable character, but he does have a code. What is it? What attitudes do the other characters have toward him? Might these attitudes be different if the story was not being told in terms of comedy?
4. How does the Marshal's marriage symbolize a turning point in the life and manners of Yellow Sky? What other details show that Yellow Sky is no longer a raw frontier town?
5. In transferring Stephen Crane's story to the screen, Agee has made several changes in the original. Below are some points in Crane's story. Discuss why Agee might have made the changes he did for the film. How have the changes contributed to the effectiveness of the film?
   a) In the story, Potter and his Bride seem to know each other fairly well and are not very shy with each other.
   b) Crane wrote: "The Bride was not pretty, nor was she very young."
   c) In the original, Scratchy is more of a tough guy, less obviously a buffoon.
   d) In the original the barkeep is a man.
6. **Contrasting characters.** The two women, Laura Lee and the Bride, are both likeable and attractive characters. How are they different? How does this contrast in character support the theme?
7. Discuss the implications of this camera direction concerning Laura Lee: "Then she realizes she is dead." (page 102)
8. **Visual symbol.** Discuss the meaning of the final camera direction: "the funnel-shaped tracks of his feet in heavy sand." What does this visual image suggest? Why does the writer want the sand to be "heavy"?

Interaction

1. **The art of the film.** The film has today been accepted as an important art form, different in its methods from "live" theater. In the early days of motion pictures (1923) T. S. Eliot worried about the decline of the living theater and the growth of the movies as popular entertainment. He thought that the audience at a live performance *participated* actively, but that the person sitting at a movie had "his mind . . . lulled by continuous senseless music and continuous action too rapid for the brain to act upon, and will receive, without giving. . . ."

   Discuss Eliot's statement drawing upon your own experience with movies, television, and live theater. Do you find that at the movies you "receive without giving"? Do you find "continuous action too rapid for the brain to act upon"? Is this necessarily bad, as Eliot suggests? Or might it be a good characteristic of film technique?

2. **Print and film.** As a special — and challenging — project, make a written or oral report comparing Agee's motion picture adaptation of "The Bride Comes to Yellow Sky" with Stephen Crane's original story. (You have already considered a few of the changes in question 5 of the **Study Guide.**) Try not to think of the changes in purely "literary" terms such as the treatment of character. Rather, think in terms of the needs of the two media: print and film. Take one or two specific moments or images which appear in both versions: How does Crane make his effect with print? How does Agee make the same effect in film?

   Here, for example, is the final scene as Crane wrote it:

   "Married?" said Scratchy. Seemingly for the first time, he saw the drooping, drowning woman at the other man's side. "No!" he said. He was like a creature allowed a glimpse of another world. He moved a pace backward, and his arm, with the revolver, dropped to his side. "Is this the lady?" he asked.
   "Yes; this is the lady," answered Potter.
   There was another period of silence.
   "Well," said Wilson at last, slowly, "I s'pose it's all off now."
   "It's all off if you say so, Scratchy. You know I didn't make the trouble." Potter lifted his valise.
   "Well, I 'low it's off, Jack," said Wilson. He was looking at the ground. "Married!" He was not a student of chivalry; it was merely that in the presence of this foreign condition he was a simple child of the earlier plains. He picked up his starboard revolver and, placing both weapons in their holsters, he went away. His feet made funnel-shaped tracks in the heavy sand.

3. James Agee's book *Agee on Film* contains an essay on moving-picture comedy, "Comedy's Greatest Era." In this essay Agee argues that the old silent comedies were funnier than those made after the "talkies" came in. "The only thing wrong with screen comedy today," he wrote, "is that it takes place on a screen which talks."

In writing this screenplay, Agee tried to avoid making a script in which the humor is purely verbal. What are some of the opportunities he gives the actors for *visual* comedy? Show how, in one or two scenes, what the audience *sees* might add to the comedy present in the dialogue.

The Flower-Fed Buffaloes

Text page 104

VACHEL LINDSAY 1879–1931

Vachel Lindsay was born in Springfield, Illinois, the town that inspired his famous poem "Abraham Lincoln Walks at Midnight." For a while he was a professional artist. Unable to sell his paintings, however, he set out on a vagabond tour of the West, trading poems for food. His poems and his stirring poetry readings made him famous as an experimenter with sound and beat in poetry. (See page 770 for the poem "General William Booth Enters into Heaven.")

Study Guide

1. Which of these three statements best describes the tone or attitude behind the poem?
   a) The speaker is angered by the passing of a landscape inhabited by the buffalo and the Indians. Civilization is a curse; he uses the wheel as a symbol of a civilization that brings about evil and destruction.
   b) The speaker is unhappy about the passing of the buffalo and the Indians as he would be at the end of anything beautiful and natural. He is not angry, however, and points no accusing finger at the white man and his civilization. The tone is one of nostalgia and quiet sadness.
   c) The speaker joyously celebrates the coming of the white man's wagons, railroads, and agriculture. The senseless violence of the wild animals and Indians is at last ended.
2. Would this poem make a good lyric for a modern folk song?

The Leader of the People

Text pages 105–119

<small>JOHN STEINBECK</small>   1902–1968

John Steinbeck was born in California, which provides the setting for many of his stories and novels, such as *East of Eden*. He attended Stanford University and then worked at various jobs, including, like Eric Hoffer, work as an itinerant fruit picker. In 1935, with the publication of *Tortilla Flat*, Steinbeck began to earn his living as a writer. Two years later, the best-selling *Of Mice and Men* made him famous. This short novel about two friends in the Depression years was later made into a Broadway play and a motion picture. Steinbeck then wrote *The Grapes of Wrath*, one of the most important American novels of the thirties. *The Grapes of Wrath* is also set during the Depression years and tells the story of the "Okies," the Oklahoma farmers who left their unproductive land to seek work as fruit pickers in California.

In his work Steinbeck often identified himself with the poor and the exploited. When the Nobel Academy awarded him the Prize for Literature in 1962, the award cited Steinbeck's sympathy for "the oppressed, the misfits, the distressed." In *The Pearl*, a short novel set in Mexico, Steinbeck again portrays the people he knows so well — people who are in a struggle for the bare necessities of life and are gripped by forces too complex for them to control. His last important work *Travels with Charlie* is in a different vein; it is a sometimes light, sometimes angry account of the author's tour of America with his dog, Charlie.

Comment

. . . Steinbeck has been astonishingly consistent. A single purpose has directed his experimentation, a single idea has guided his literary thought. Always his fiction has described the interplay of dream and reality; his thought has followed the development of the American dream.

— FREDERICK I. CARPENTER: John Steinbeck:
American Dreamer

Study Guide

1. **Character.** Authors do not usually stop to give their readers a complete description of a character. The reader looks at the things a character says, does, and thinks, and a general impression of the character forms in his mind.

   What do we learn about Jody's dreams and yearnings from this description?

   Jody lay in his bed and thought of the impossible world of Indians and buffaloes, a world that had ceased to be forever. He wished he could have been living in the heroic time, but he knew he was not of heroic timber. No one living now, save possibly Billy Buck, was worthy to do the things that had been done. A race of giants had lived then, fearless men, men of a staunchness unknown in this day. (page 115)

   Steinbeck also shows a streak of cruelty in Jody, a desire for violence and destruction. This side of Jody is shown in little things he does: throwing a stone at some birds (page 105); thinking with satisfaction that the mice "would not survive another day." (page 106) Does Steinbeck make Jody a mean, vicious boy? In what way is Jody's violent side an expression of his dreams and yearnings?

2. Grandfather clings to his memories of the excitement and danger of the frontier. Why is he closer to Jody than to any other character in the story? How do the others — Billy Buck, Carl, and the mother — treat the grandfather?

3. Grandfather regrets that his stories irritate Carl. Even more, though, he regrets the fact that "Westering has died out of the people." (page 119) Does this statement apply to Carl Tiflin?

   Carl is the most unsympathetic character in the story. Grandfather was a leader and Jody dreams of being a leader. How does Carl attempt to satisfy a longing to lead? See, for example, such clues as, "His father, Carl Tiflin, insisted upon giving permission for anything that was done on the ranch, whether it was important or not" (page 106) and " 'He *is* getting to be a Big-Britches,' Carl said. 'He's minding everybody's business but his own. Got his big nose into everything.' " (page 107)

4. At the end of the story, Jody feels sad about Grandfather's final disillusionment. How does Jody show his understanding and sympathy? Earlier, Jody had decided that "he was not of heroic timber." (page 115) Do you agree?

Interaction

1. Discuss the implications of Grandfather's words: "Westering has died out of the people. Westering isn't a hunger any more. It's all done." (page 119) In what sense is this true? In what sense false? How does Jody react to Grandfather's statement that "There's no place to go"?
2. Compare Eric Hoffer's ideas about the characters and motives of the pioneers with those of Grandfather in the story. Are the two positions entirely in disagreement?

The Meaning of the Frontier: Summing Up

1. This section is called "The Meaning of the Frontier." In the introduction you read that the section was not about the "real" West, but about the meaning the western frontier has had in the American imagination. What are some of the meanings the frontier had for the following authors or characters?
   a) Mark Twain ("The Pony Express")
   b) John Colter
   c) Lester ("Strong Men, Riding Horses")
   d) Scratchy ("The Bride Comes to Yellow Sky")
   e) Eric Hoffer
   f) Jody ("The Leader of the People")
   g) Grandfather ("The Leader of the People")
2. Consider the following quotation from Marshall McLuhan: "The past went that-a-way. When faced with a totally new situation, we tend always to attach ourselves to the objects, to the flavor of the most recent past. We look back at the present through a rear-view mirror. We march backward into the future. Suburbia lives imaginatively in Bonanza-land." (Note: At the time Mc-Luhan wrote these words, *Bonanza* was one of America's favorite television programs: a typical romantic-heroic view of the West.)

   Discuss "Our Romantic View of the Frontier." Refer to Mc-Luhan's remark if you wish. More important, draw examples to support your ideas from the selections you have read in this section.

AMERICAN HUMOR

As you will see in Hawthorne's stories about Puritan times, humor was not much prized among the Puritans. The picture we have of them as stern, God-fearing people may at times be overdrawn but is essentially true. A Puritan minister who wrote a satire on manners in 1646 was frowned upon, and later, in New Jersey, the state legislature requested the Governor to conduct official business without joking.

But humor is an irrepressible part of human nature. As American attitudes relaxed, humor quickly came out into the open. An early, and still classic, example of written humor was Ben Franklin's *Poor Richard's Almanack*. Many of the "folk sayings" of Poor Richard had a humorous twist to them: "Three may keep a secret, if two of them are dead."

DIALECT HUMOR AND THE TALL TALE

Most of the humor of nineteenth-century America was rural in character and leaned heavily on a use of American dialects. The cracker-barrel philosopher, the Yankee peddler, the trickster, the medicine man, the sharp farm hand — all were familiar types on the stage and in print. Mark Twain's Tom Sawyer is a descendant of these rogues. In order to imitate spoken language in print, dialect humorists liked to use misspellings. Josh Billings's "Essa on the Muel" on page 123 is a good — and blessedly brief — example of this kind of writing. We no longer find misspellings and mispronunciations as funny as our ancestors did. But dialect humor is still good for a laugh — if not for a fight.

Along with dialect humor, the tall tale should be mentioned as an important strain in American humor. Folk humor all over the world has always depended for its effect upon exaggeration. The American frontiersman, however, carried exaggeration to new heights. Men like Davy Crockett popularized the tall tale, with stories like the one about the man who bent his rifle so that he could shoot around the corner.

THE WRITER AS COMEDIAN

The mid-nineteenth century was the age of "literary comedians," traveling lecturers like Artemus Ward and Mark Twain. Ward would come on stage, glum, nervous, and embarrassed; he spoke in

Yankee dialect, looking faintly surprised and deadly serious when the audience laughed at his wisecracks. Ward made the "dead pan" an important part of American humor.

Mark Twain, who, of course, was more than a humorist, learned the "dead pan" from Ward. Twain combined and perfected the various strains in American humor. His Tom Sawyer is a typical "shifty rogue" and Huck Finn a typical unschooled but nevertheless wise narrator. Twain brought together cracker-barrel philosophy, the tall tale, and dialect in "The Story of the Old Ram." American storytelling also was casual and meandering rather than logically structured, and Twain's "The Story of the Old Ram" is a classic "wandering tale." This tradition continues in Thurber's "University Days" (page 125 of the anthology), written a century later.

The rise of the cities and the narrowing of the frontier after the Civil War brought changes to American humor. The feeling for the spoken language remained, with hillbilly, Brooklyn, Irish, Jewish, and Negro intonations being added to the southwestern and Yankee drawls. One of the most readable of immigrant humorists is Finley Peter Dunne, whose Mr. Dooley commented on politics in a thick Irish brogue.

A great deal of modern humor grows out of the tradition of dialect humor and the tall tale. Witness the popularity of television shows about hillbillies and wisely innocent rural folk. Another and very different strain is the ironic humor discussed in the Introduction on page 122 of the anthology. This harsh, biting humor contrasts with the gentle, more forgiving humor of "The Story of the Old Ram" and *Old Times on the Mississippi.*

Essa on the Muel

Text pages 123–124

JOSH BILLINGS   1818–1885

Henry Wheeler Shaw, who wrote under the penname Josh Billings, tried his hand at several professions before becoming a writer in his late forties. He was at various times a farmer, coal operator, real estate dealer, auctioneer, and, like Mark Twain, a steamboat pilot. He then became one of the many early American humorists who entertained audiences with their "lectures" and wrote newspaper columns in outrageous spelling.

Study Guide

1. What human qualities does Billings give the mule? Why does the mule look for "a good chanse to kick sumbody"?
2. "Yu hav tew be wise before yu kan be witty," Billings wrote. What "wise" observation does the narrator make about the human race in general? What comments does he make about specific groups of people?
3. Besides misspellings, Billings uses the following devices to entertain his readers:
   a) *malapropism:* an absurd misuse of words.
   b) *comparisons* with homely and familiar objects.
   c) *anticlimax:* a sudden unimportant or derogatory statement after an impressive statement; a drop from the sublime to the ridiculous.
   d) *tall tale:* an extravagant, exaggerated story.

   What examples of these devices do you find in "Essa on the Muel"?

Interaction

1. People respond to the dialect humor in "Essa on the Muel" in many different ways. Did you find it uproariously funny? mildly amusing? or interesting only as a specimen of nineteenth-century dialect humor?

   One of the most difficult kinds of literary discussion is an explanation of why you find something funny or unfunny. Bearing in mind this difficulty, try to explain your reaction to "Essa on the Muel."

2. E. B. White, a modern humorist and essayist, has discussed the kind of dialect humor Josh Billings liked to use:

   Not long ago I plunged back fifty to a hundred years into this school of dialect humor that Mark Twain found perishable. Then was the heyday of the cracker-barrel philosopher, sometimes wise, always wise-seeming, and when read today rather dreary. It seemed to me, in reading the dialect boys, that a certain basic confusion often exists in the use of tricky or quaint or illiterate spelling to achieve a humorous effect. I mean, it is not always clear whether the author intends his character to be writing or speaking — and I, for one, feel that unless I know at least this much about what I am reading, I am off to a bad start. For instance, here are some spellings from the works of Petroleum V. Nasby: he spells "would" *wood*, "of" *uv*, "you" *yoo*, "hence" *hentz*, "office" *offis*.

Now, it happens that I pronounce "office" *offis*. And I pronounce "hence" *hentz*, and I even pronounce "of" *uv*. Therefore, I infer that Nasby's character is supposed not to be speaking but to be writing. Yet in either event, justification for this perversion of the language is lacking; for if the character is speaking, the queer spelling is unnecessary, since the pronunciation is almost indistinguishable from the natural or ordinary pronunciation, and if the character is writing, the spelling is most unlikely. Who ever wrote "uv" for "of"? Nobody. Anyone who knows how to write at all knows how to spell a simple word like "of." If you can't spell "of" you wouldn't be able to spell anything and wouldn't be attempting to set words to paper — much less words like "solissitood." A person who can't spell "of" is an illiterate, and the only time such a person attempts to write anything down is in a great crisis. He doesn't write political essays or diaries or letters or satirical paragraphs.

· · ·

I suspect that the popularity of all dialect stuff derives in part from flattery of the reader — giving him a pleasant sensation of superiority which he gets from working out the intricacies of misspelling, and the satisfaction of detecting boorishness or illiteracy in someone else. This is not the whole story but it has some bearing in the matter. Incidentally, I am told by an authority on juvenile literature that dialect is tops with children. They like to puzzle out the words. When they catch on to the thing, they must feel that first fine glow of maturity — the ability to exercise higher intellectual powers than those of the character they are looking at.

E. B. White's first point is that misspellings in dialect humor indicate that the narrator is writing, not speaking. White says that if he were speaking, the misspellings would be unnecessary; and that if he were really as illiterate as his spelling implies, he wouldn't be writing. Did this "basic confusion" bother you when you read Billings's "Essa"? White's second point is that dialect humor flatters us, makes us feel superior to the speaker. Do you agree or disagree?

3. Dialect, as has been said, has long been a standard element in American humor. However, at various times some people have found dialect offensive because it appears to ridicule groups from certain geographical, national, or racial backgrounds. Some groups enjoy dialect humor at their own expense when used by a member of their own group, but they resent it from outsiders.

Consider some of the popular television programs and comedians you are familiar with. Which depend in some measure upon dialect humor? Do you find the use of dialect offensive?

University Days

Text pages 125–131

JAMES THURBER 1894–1961

James Thurber entered Ohio State in 1913. Blind in one eye since childhood, he later in life became totally blind. For much of his career as a writer Thurber was associated with the *New Yorker* magazine as an editor, essayist, short-story writer, and cartoonist. He became noted for his blend of wit and pathos in such stories as "The Secret Life of Walter Mitty." Thurber often uses the fable and the fairy tale as humorous forms, and his subjects generally include the helpless hero and the battle of the sexes. Some of his humorous works are *The Owl in the Attic and Other Perplexities; My Life and Hard Times; Cream of Thurber; The Beast in Me; Thurber Country; Men, Women, and Dogs;* and *The Male Animal* (a play).

Comment

There is an eerie, zany quality about his humor that hides a shiver under the laugh. He is consciously whistling in a graveyard: and the terror — which we all share — behind the mirth makes the mirth just so much the funnier.

— STANLEY J. KUNITZ *and* HOWARD HAYCRAFT:
Twentieth Century Authors

Study Guide

1. Like Twain's "wandering tale," Thurber's essay describes many incidents which seem unrelated at first glance. The basic source of the humor here is the discrepancy between what we expect of a great university and the trivial, mindless activities that actually go on. What are some of these trivial, mindless activities?
2. General Littlefield tells Thurber, "You are the main trouble with this university." In what sense was Thurber "trouble"? Thurber's tone is rather sorrowful, as if at the time he regretted not being able to conform. Is the older Thurber sorry that as a young man he couldn't conform? Explain.

3. Thurber frequently uses dialogue to allow the characters themselves to show how laughable they are. What amusing foibles do the characters reveal in their dialogue? What does Thurber laugh at in himself?
4. Thurber speaks of the "anguish" of those college days. In what ways was it "anguish"? Do you think "anguish" is an exaggeration? Why or why not? In what ways were Thurber's university days interesting and amusing?

Interaction

1. It has been said that Thurber's "whimsy conceals deadly satire." Judging from "University Days," do you agree? Why or why not?
2. Try writing an informal essay in the light and humorous manner of Thurber about your own school days.

Ambition

Text page 131

Morris Bishop   *born:* 1893

For many years Morris Bishop has been a teacher of French and Spanish at Cornell University. He has written biographies of explorers and philosophers as well as volumes of humorous poetry. He also wrote a mystery, *The Widening Stain,* under the penname W. Bolingbroke Johnson. Bishop expressed his philosophy of light verse in the Preface to *A Bowl of Bishop:* "The appreciation of light verse depends on the appreciation of heavy verse." He feels that the audience for poetry is growing smaller every day. As for his own poetry, Bishop has written:

> Many a man has read my rhymes and did not like a word of 'em;
> And very many more there be who never even heard of 'em.
> I do not mind if you should find these poems misbegotten;
> "It's all a question of taste," I'd say, "and your taste is rotten."

Study Guide

1. What sort of person is Bishop laughing at in "Ambition"?
2. What unusual rhymes does he use? Which ones would be out of place in "serious" verse?
3. What does the last line imply? What does Bishop say about competitiveness in this poem?

"Take the Witness!"

Text pages 132–134

ROBERT BENCHLEY   1889–1945

Robert Benchley has been called the most "versatile humorist in America" because he worked in so many media: newspapers, magazines, radio, and movies. He also performed on the stage, delivering comic monologues. His humor has been described as "a fresh, naive humor which possesses much point but no sting."

Comment

The funny people you like best are the ones you laugh *with*. There's Benchley, for instance. You live through his troubles with him — they are your own troubles — and that is why you enjoy them so particularly.   — DOROTHY PARKER

Study Guide

1. Benchley's clever remarks to the lawyer would simply be wisecracks without the "real" Benchley, the one talking to us. This contrast between the real and the imagined is the key to Benchley's humor here. What universal human tendency is Benchley commenting on?
2. **Understatement.** Subtle humorists often use understatement instead of exaggeration. They deliberately seem gentle, casual, and restrained while laughing at something. Thurber, in "University Days," never says bluntly that the football tackle was stupid; instead he says, ". . . while he was not dumber than an ox he was not any smarter." What examples of understatement do you find in " 'Take the Witness!' "?
3. What does Benchley say would happen if he ever had to take the stand in real life? Do you agree with him? What is Benchley's attitude toward himself in the essay — does he take himself seriously and laugh at others, or does he poke fun at himself too?

Interaction

Thomas Lask writes that Thurber and Benchley have unusual qualities as humorists: "They are not sour, or cruel, or unkind." Do you agree?

There is a similarity between *humor* and *satire*. Both forms use comic devices, both laugh at human foibles. There are differences, however, in tone and purpose. The satirist is often "sour, or cruel, or unkind." He thinks that by scolding and ridiculing humanity he can change society. The humorist laughs, but he has no great ambition to correct mankind's behavior. Consider " 'Take the Witness!' " along with the other selections in this section on American humor. Consider also "The Story of the Old Ram" (page 3) and "The Bride Comes to Yellow Sky" (page 68). Do any of these selections, or do any parts of these selections, fit the description of satire better than the description of humor? Explain your answer.

Love Is a Fallacy

Text pages 135–145

MAX SHULMAN   *born:* 1919

Max Shulman began writing at the University of Minnesota, where he majored in journalism and edited the humor magazine. The year after he graduated, he published his first novel, *Barefoot Boy with Cheek*, a comedy of college life. He has since written other books on "university days," including *The Many Loves of Dobie Gillis* and *I Was a Teen-Age Dwarf*. His novel *Rally Round the Flag, Boys* satirizes the "brave new plastic world" of suburbia. Shulman's humor is noted for its puns, outrageous names (Asa Hearthrug, Yetta Samovar) and wild coincidences. Many of his stories have been adapted for television and movies.

Study Guide

1. The narrator tells us, "Look at me — a brilliant student, a tremendous intellectual, a man with an assured future." What in the story contradicts his high opinion of himself?
2. Why is the narrator interested in Polly? Why is he interested in logic? Does he believe that logic can be applied to life? Use quotations from the story to support your answers.
3. Petey and Polly talk alike; both use all the current campus slang. What campus types is Shulman poking fun at in Petey and Polly? The narrator's speech is not slangy; in fact, he has a rather lofty way of talking, which adds to the humor: "I had long coveted

Polly Espy"; "I had gravely underestimated the size of my task"; "The dear child had learned her lessons perhaps too well." What campus type does Shulman satirize in his characterization of the narrator?

4. Shulman brings his story to an end with a surprising twist. Why did the narrator's carefully worked out, logical plan of action backfire — was Petey at all responsible? Or was the narrator himself responsible? Or was the illogic known as "feminine logic" responsible?

5. Why is the ending amusing instead of sad?

Interaction

1. The stereotype of women as less logical and intelligent, more emotional and impulsive than men is a result of fallacious thinking. In what ways does Polly fit the stereotype? How does it work to her advantage?

2. "Love Is a Fallacy" and "University Days" were written at a time when campus life seemed to be a carefree, gently goofy period in young people's lives. Does the view of college life presented in these two selections correspond to young people's concerns and activities on campuses today? Explain your answer with specific examples.

3. Comedy has traditionally been thought of as having a happy ending. "Love Is a Fallacy" does not have a happy ending in the traditional sense, because the hero does not get the girl at the end of the story. Instead, he gets a kind of poetic justice. The ending is ironic rather than comic. What would be lost if Shulman had given the story a traditionally happy ending?

The Day the T.V. Broke

Text page 146

GERALD JONAS *born:* 1935

Gerald Jonas has worked as a writer and reporter for the *New Yorker* since 1961. He is also a free-lance writer of poems and science fiction. "Science-fiction poems," he writes, "are a particular favorite of mine, and I like to think that 'The Day the T.V. Broke' has a science-fiction flavor."

Study Guide

1. What has television done to the poet's life? How did the T.V. breakdown affect him psychologically?
2. Is the last line of the poem in praise or in criticism of television? Explain your answer.
3. What do you think is the point of this poem?

Love Song

Text page 147

Dorothy Parker   1893–1967

Dorothy Parker was one of the few American writers to have a book of verse on the best-seller list. Along with Thurber, E. B. White, and other writers for the *New Yorker*, she became known as one of the New York Wits, whose style was urbane, casual, and conversational. The subject of Dorothy Parker poems and stories is frequently heartbreak, which she often treats with irony. She is famous for such classic quips as the two-line poem: "Men seldom make passes/At girls who wear glasses." Some of her works are *Enough Rope, Death and Taxes,* and *Collected Stories.*

Study Guide

1. Dorothy Parker often wrote cynically about love and romance. How does she feel about her "own dear love"?
2. How does the last line of each stanza differ from the previous lines?
3. Which lines and phrases paint an exaggerated romantic picture? How does Dorothy Parker deflate this exaggerated picture?
4. Dorothy Parker's poems have been called "bittersweet" and "more bitter than sweet." Do you agree with this statement? Why or why not?

Interaction

1. Each of the poems in this unit — "Ambition," "The Day the T.V. Broke," and "Love Song" — belongs to a class of literature called light verse. Another example in the anthology is Morris Bishop's "Phaethon" on page 227. Judging from these four poems, how do you think light verse differs from "serious" verse in content? in technique?

2. Light verse can be written in either strictly regular form (like Dorothy Parker's "Love Song") or in a very free form (like "The Day the T.V. Broke" and "Ambition"). Using either the regular or the free form, try your hand at some light verse commenting on some human foible. Try to use rhyme to enhance the comic effect.

American Humor: Summing Up

1. Mark Twain in his later years said, "Humor must not professedly teach, and it must not professedly preach, but it must do both if it would live forever. By forever I mean thirty years." E. B. White disagrees with Twain: "I don't think I agree that humor must preach in order to live; it need only speak the truth — and I notice it usually does." Max Shulman, in one of his rare serious moments in print, wrote that American humor clowns at the expense of truth. Bearing in mind the opinions of these humorists, do you think it is necessary for a humorous work to make a point — a true observation about people?

   Look again at one or two of the following selections in the anthology. Does the author have a point to make? Does he give us an insight into the way people really are? Or is he interested simply in having a good time?
   a) "The Story of the Old Ram" (page 3)
   b) *Old Times on the Mississippi* (page 14)
   c) "The Bride Comes to Yellow Sky" (page 68)
   d) "Essa on the Muel" (page 123)
   e) "University Days" (page 125)
   f) " 'Take the Witness!' " (page 132)
   g) "Love Is a Fallacy" (page 135)
   h) the humorous poems (pages 131; 146–147)
2. A contemporary humorist says, "A sense of humor means that you can laugh at yourself." In which of the selections in this section does the speaker or writer make fun of himself? In which selection or selections do we laugh at a speaker who takes himself very seriously?

THE AMERICAN LANGUAGE

Americans have never formalized the American language. The French set up an academy to standardize rules of grammar, and in England Samuel Johnson and Jonathan Swift tried to expurgate words like *fun, stingy, mob,* and *bully* from British English. But no one has ever set up permanent rules for "correctness" in American English. Our standard of correctness is based on usage, not rules. Even though we become conscious of "correctness" in certain situations, such as the classroom or formal gatherings, Americans are used to hearing and reading many varieties of American English. Television, radio, and films have accustomed us to different accents. Furthermore, we admire writers like Twain who have a keen ear for regional dialect and colloquial prose.

The selections and **Study Guides** in this unit, therefore, are not aimed at setting down rules for "correct" usage. Rather, they describe the way Americans talk, the way we think about language, and the way our language has been influenced by tradition, geography, and time.

America Talking

Text pages 152–160

Bergen Evans *born:* 1904

Bergen Evans has written many books and dictionaries, including *Comfortable Words* and, in collaboration with his sister, Cornelia Evans, *A Dictionary of Contemporary American Usage.* Dr. Evans is Professor of English at Northwestern University.

Dialect is a word you have come across before, in your study of Twain, in the section on American humor, and now in "America Talking." A *dialect* is a variation from the standard language. The people who speak it can usually be identified with a particular community or geographical area. A *dialect* differs from the standard language in at least three ways: vocabulary, pronunciation, and cadence. Professor Evans, in *A Dictionary of Contemporary American*

Usage, tells something about the attitudes Americans have toward dialect:

Where a dialect is native, there is nothing wrong in this; indeed, it often confers a pleasing distinction. But, unfortunately, snobbery sometimes attaches opprobrium to some dialects. . . . Outside of the community where such dialects prevail, even a tincture of them may do a man harm. It's cruel, but that is the way of the as-yet-imperfect world.

Study Guide

1. What attitude does the author take toward the regional differences in American speech? What advantage does he find in these differences? what disadvantages? In what direction does he think American speech differences are moving?
2. The author describes some of Dr. Henry Lee Smith's tests for determining through pronunciation where a person comes from. Test the pronunciation of these words on yourself, your classmates, and friends. Try to account for and interpret the differences and similarities. Is Dr. Smith's description borne out by your test?
    a) merry, marry, Mary
    b) water, wash
    c) on, off, dog, sorry
    d) father, part, park
    e) about the house
    f) greasy

    If a tape recorder is available, use it for this exercise. In judging your own speech in particular, the tape recorder will give you more objectivity.
3. Among the many specific examples Evans gives, there are probably a few that you can check against your own experience. For those that you *can* check, do you find his statements correct? For example: If you are from Vermont, do you really hear the word *yallop* used to describe a dog's bark? Do Southerners really use *you-all* (or y'all) only as a plural? What about "the coast"? Do people mean only Los Angeles by this expression?
4. The author says that the broad *a* of British English in such words as *glass*, *path*, and *dance* became a shibboleth for the colonists when they began to seek independence. What is a shibboleth? What is its derivation? Can you cite other words or sounds of British English which Americans "resent" — or do you disagree with the author that there is any such resentment?

Interaction

1. Find examples of dialect or regional speech in some of the following selections in this book:
    a) "The Story of the Old Ram" (page 3)
    b) *Old Times on the Mississippi* (page 14)
    c) "The Outcasts of Poker Flat" (page 44)
    d) "The Bride Comes to Yellow Sky" (page 68)
2. Oliver Wendell Holmes said: "A word is not a crystal, transparent and unchanging; it is the skin of a living thought and may vary greatly in color and content according to the circumstances and time in which it is used." Find examples in this essay to support Holmes's statement.

Slurvian Self-Taught

Text pages 161–163

JOHN DAVENPORT *born:* 1904

John Davenport is a reporter and editor who often writes on economics.

Almost every language is freer in its spoken form than in its written form. For example, you may automatically use slang when you talk, but usually when you write you use standard American English.

Study Guide

1. **Definition by example.** What distinguishes the Slurvian words from the English words in the following list?

Yerpeen	European
nittly	in Italy
Hard	Howard
claps	collapse
surp	syrup
airs	errors

Can you add some others to the list? If you can see the differences and can add other examples to the list, then you have a clear understanding of what Davenport means by "Slurvian."

2. Understanding a writer's point of view is mainly a matter of recognizing his assumptions, his standards. What assumptions does Davenport make about language, the pronunciation of language, American society, and American education?
3. **Tone.** What do you think the author accomplishes by using the pseudo-scholarly tone of a highly educated intellectual who is so fascinated by Slurvian that he is "compiling a dictionary" which will be the "definitive work on the subject"? Would the essay have been more effective if Davenport told you directly that he thinks Slurvian is funny?

Interaction

1. This question asks you to make your own value judgment. (Since it is a value judgment, there is no way to "prove" that you are right or wrong; however, discussion of different points of view may be instructive.) Do you think that Slurvian is something to be combated? Or do you think that it should be accepted like all other forms of language change? Why?
2. We do not pronounce all of the letters in thousands of English words: Christmas, gnat, marriage, know, whole, etc. Why do these words not qualify for the Slurvian dictionary?

Different Cultural Levels Eat Here

Text pages 164–170

PETER DE VRIES   *born:* 1910

Peter De Vries was born in Chicago, Illinois. After graduating from college, he worked on his neighborhood newspaper, operated candy vending machines, sold taffy apples, and acted on radio. He then became an associate editor for *Poetry*, and through this magazine met James Thurber, who persuaded him to write for the *New Yorker*. Several novels followed De Vries's move to New York, such as *Reuben, Reuben* and *Let Me Count the Ways*. De Vries's writing is a mixture of offbeat humor and pathos, of puns and tragicomedy.

Whenever you speak, you tell your listener more than just the sense of your words. Your accent, your tone, your vocabulary, and your pace say a lot too. Your speech may tell your listener something about yourself: where you were raised, how much money you make, how much education you've had, and how tuned in you are to the latest fads in conversation. *Mit* and *mitout* in De Vries's story, then, are more than simply ways of ordering or not ordering onions.

Study Guide

1. Although this story is generally comic in tone, it is also a poignant description of the way in which "cultural levels" may act as barriers between people. Who is actually more sophisticated and sensitive in the use of language — the counterman or the four customers? Why? Why does the counterman make the customers uneasy and nervous? Why do they make him nervous?
2. Why does the proprietor, Al, use fancy phrases like "intelligent human beings" and "different cultural levels" in speaking to the four customers?
3. **Connotation.** "I know what wonderful means," the counterman says. "You don't have to tell me." Do he and the woman with the gardenia really understand the word in the same way? If so, why is he offended?
4. **Conflict.** What is the real cause of tension between the counterman and the four customers? Is it language? or something else? Explain.
5. When the fifth customer comes in, why does the counterman suddenly change to "Onion with these"? Why does he switch back to "Mit or mitout?" at the end of the story?
6. One of the functions of language is to show that we *belong* to a certain group. How is this shown at the end of the story when Louie comes into the diner?

Interaction

1. In your opinion, was the counterman too "touchy"? How could he have handled the situation better? Was there a failure of communication on his part? Explain.

2. Look again at the following selections. What does the characters' use of language show about their "cultural levels"?
   a) "The Story of the Old Ram" (page 3)
   b) "The Bride Comes to Yellow Sky" (page 68)
   c) "The Leader of the People" (page 105)
3. How might a phrase like *mit or mitout?* be used as a shibboleth? (See anthology page 153.)

The American Folk Song

Text pages 171–177

OSCAR BRAND   born: 1920

Oscar Brand has immersed himself in every aspect of our American folk music heritage. He is a singer, songwriter, scholar, and one of the people responsible for the folk music revival in America. During World War II he used folk music as therapy for hospitalized servicemen. Later he became a professional folk singer, saying, "It's easier than working for a living." He has adapted traditional folk music to popular songs and soundtracks for motion pictures and commercials. And for his radio shows, T.V. programs, and concerts, he has sought in every section of the country for that "simple, traditional sound" we associate with folk music.

Oscar Brand was born in Manitoba, Canada, to a family of traveling singers. After graduation from high school, he roamed around the U.S. with his banjo, earning his living by farm work. He then entered Brooklyn College to take his degree in psychology. During World War II he received a citation for his work with the wounded. Through his songs, scholarly and humorous essays, and performances in every medium, he has become an important interpreter of our folk music heritage.

Ballads, Spirituals, and Blues

Text pages 178–183

American dialects have been made vivid in the works of writers like Mark Twain. They have also been preserved by the very people who spoke them — especially in their songs. These songs may tell a story, express an emotion, or celebrate a religious belief. Each song creates its own mood. How would you describe the underlying mood of each song? What words helped convey this mood?

Jesse James. Jesse James used the alias "Howard." Hence the chorus: "that dirty little coward that shot Mr. Howard,/Has laid Jesse James in his grave."

The song makes no pretense that Jesse James was not a murderer and a train robber. Yet he is portrayed in a sympathetic light, and the song appears to be almost a lament for his death. Why should the anonymous maker of this song have any sympathy for Jesse James? Why would the millions of people who have helped make the song famous share this ambiguous attitude — seeing him as both a criminal and a hero?

Go Down, Moses. During the era of slavery, when many of the spirituals were composed, these songs often had a double meaning. In some sense they were expressions of religious feelings; in another, they were songs of protest. In "Go Down, Moses" the connection is clear: it was easy for the slaves to see a parallel between their bondage and that of the Children of Israel held captive by the Pharaohs.

Backwater Blues. Floods, like the one described in this song, often hit the poor harder than they hit the rich. In many communities the well-to-do could afford higher land.

Mean and Evil Woman Blues. In an interesting essay on the blues, S. I. Hayakawa points out that the lyrics of the blues usually take a "realistic" attitude toward love, as does the singer in this song when he says "I ain't gonna let you worry my life no more." Hayakawa points out that the lyrics to well-known old standards usually take a more sentimental view, with such thoughts as "Some day my Prince will come!" But in recent years the influence of such musicians as Bob Dylan and the Beatles has toughened the attitudes expressed in popular music.

Ballads, Spirituals, and Blues: Interaction

1. In "The Role of the Undesirables" in the section on "The Meaning of the Frontier," Eric Hoffer has described the migrant worker camp as a human junkpile. He describes the migrants as cripples,

drunks, loafers, fugitives from justice, and mental defectives. Among such men unfulfilled dreams and ambitions, personal tragedies and failures must have been numerous. Imagine yourself to be one of them and attempt to put some of your thoughts and feelings into the form of a blues song or ballad.

2. Whitman's poem "Texas Massacre" (page 65) is essentially a narrative and similar to the narrative aspect of many ballads. Retell the events of Whitman's narrative in ballad form. What changes become necessary?

3. Write a ballad about Scratchy in "The Bride Comes to Yellow Sky" or John Oakhurst in "The Outcasts of Poker Flat."

4. After you have listened to some records of ballads and blues to get the "feel" of these songs, try your hand at writing some of your own. Model your work on that of any of your favorite folk singers. You may wish to base your song on a modern theme; you can find material in the daily paper, in the life around you, or in your own experience.

NATHANIEL HAWTHORNE 1804–1864

"For a long, long while," Nathaniel Hawthorne wrote in his *Notebooks* for December 1854, "I have been visited with a singular dream . . . one of the effects of that heavy seclusion in which I shut myself up, for twelve years, after leaving college, when everybody moved onward and left me behind. How strange that it should come now . . . still that same dream of life hopelessly a failure." It was true that many of Hawthorne's friends and classmates had moved onward since the day he returned to his family's home in Salem, Massachusetts, where he had been born in 1804, to begin a long and solitary apprenticeship as an author. Franklin Pierce was now the fourteenth President of the United States. Henry Wadsworth Longfellow had become a Harvard professor and a poet of national reputation. The nation itself had moved its frontier to the Pacific; Americans, dreaming of progress and success, had turned away from the ideals of their Puritan and Revolutionary ancestors. But as a young man of twenty-one, Hawthorne chose to remain in the same town where his Puritan ancestors had settled almost two hundred years before. In his stories and novels he pondered the American past, examined the problem of moral responsibility, and confronted the question of evil.

On the surface, Hawthorne's life was uneventful. He was thirty-three before he emerged from his "dismal chamber" where "FAME was won" to publish his first collection of short stories. For a while he lived with a colony of social reformers at Brook Farm, but the communal life did not suit his skeptical temperament. At thirty-eight he married and moved to Concord, where he was a neighbor of Emerson, the transcendental philosopher whose positive view of life seemed to contradict his own. There, in 1850, he finished *The Scarlet Letter*, a novel of Puritan America, which has remained one of the masterpieces of our literature.

Even with such successful books, it was difficult for Hawthorne to make a living as a writer of fiction. He worked at various times as a journalist and as a surveyor at the customhouses in Boston and Salem. And at the height of his creative power he took a position at the American consulate in Liverpool, England, to provide for his family. His last years, before his death in 1864, were darkened by his inability to finish several novels he had started.

At first, Americans did not understand the importance of Hawthorne's stories. They saw him as a pleasant storyteller with a pleasant style, not as a serious artist who examined the human heart. But Herman Melville, the other great American novelist of the time, objected: "In one word, the world is mistaken in this Nathaniel Hawthorne. He is immeasurably deeper than the plummet of the mere critic. For it is not the brain that can test such a man; it is only the heart."

Comments

He is infinitely too fond of allegory, and can never hope for popularity so long as he persists in it.   — EDGAR ALLAN POE

Nothing is more curious and interesting than this almost exclusively *imported* character of the sense of sin in Hawthorne's mind; it seems to exist there merely for an artistic or literary purpose.
                                        — HENRY JAMES: Hawthorne

Hawthorne recognized the difference between Puritanism as a way of life and Puritanism as a scheme for dealing with reality so that it might be shaped into art. Hawthorne's home life was not puritanic, and Hawthorne's fiction builds on the Puritan system but is not used by it; the author was a creative writer, not a theological illustrator. Nothing shows the literary control he exerted over his Puritan themes more clearly than "The Maypole of Merry Mount," which begins by setting up a contrast between the pagan revelry of the Maypole celebrants and the gloomy grind of life of the Puritan settlement. It is clear that the author endorses neither view of life, but it is equally clear that in the absence of a third alternative — an absence which was not necessarily felt in the world in which Hawthorne ate his breakfast and took walking trips in the Berkshires — the Puritans' way is preferable. The trouble which comes to Merry Mount is inevitable, not because the Puritans will eventually strike, but because the revelers are men and carry their sinfulness with them regardless of whether they are afflicted from without or within. The note of doom is struck in advance of the Puritan raid by the very nature of the Lord and Lady of the May: "Alas, for the young lovers! No sooner had their hearts glowed with real passion than they were sensible of something vague and unsubstantial in their former pleasures, and felt a dreary presentiment of inevitable change. From the moment that they truly loved, they had subjected themselves to earth's doom of care and sorrow, and troubled joy, and had no more a home at Merry Mount." John Endicott's unrushing band, then, is but a public confirmation of an inner change and seals the lovers' recognition that they were born, like all humans, to an inheritance of sin.

The Puritan community in the works of Hawthorne, as "The Maypole" shows, serves as a metaphor of the corruption of man. To be sure, man's inherited sinfulness is not the whole of his make-up, but no life can be understood without taking it into account. The Puritan community in Hawthorne's fiction is consistently revealed as an unduly severe and undesirable residence, one which has exaggerated the sinful part until it dominates the whole. But it is a symbolic realization of the inescapable portion of life which those who would live life as if men were perfectible and evil an error in calculation must accept.

— LARZER ZIFF: The Artist and Puritanism

The Maypole of Merry Mount

Text pages 187–197

In a preface to the story, Hawthorne said that the historical facts he used turned into "a sort of allegory." In an allegory there is always at least one level of meaning beyond the surface of the story. Details from the literal story become "emblems" or symbols.

In this story the literal level is the conflict between the Puritans and the people of Merry Mount. Hawthorne clearly states the theme of the allegorical level in the first paragraph: "Jollity and gloom were contending for an empire." What was the empire? Literally it was New England, or perhaps America. Allegorically, the empire is the human heart. The revelers are also emblems of "idle pleasures," whereas the Puritans represent "the sternest cares of life."

Study Guide

1. Describe the setting of the opening scene of the story. Why are the people of Merry Mount gathered around the maypole? Why do the Puritans come to Merry Mount?
2. Hawthorne interrupts the marriage ceremony with several "authentic passages from history" so that we may learn who these

people really were. How does the background and outlook of the revelers differ from that of the Puritans? Besides the religious issue, list other sources of the conflict.

3. Notice that the "grizzly saints" are wearing suits of iron while the "gay sinners" are dressed in lavish silk. What are some of the other ways in which Hawthorne contrasts the opposing forces?

4. Hawthorne says: "The future complexion of New England was involved in this important quarrel." Who won? How did this victory affect the future complexion of New England?

5. Notice that the story takes place between the beginning and ending of a sunset. How do the images of light and darkness reflect the theme of the story?

6. What kind of justice does Endicott show toward the revelers? the English priest? the dancing bear? the young lovers?

7. How were Edith and Edgar different from the other people of Merry Mount? What shows that Endicott softened toward the lovers? How do you explain this softened attitude? What was the fate of the young lovers?

8. Hawthorne says that the Puritans, though "men of iron," were also "dismal wretches." On the other hand he suggests that the mirth of Merry Mount was a "counterfeit of happiness." How does Hawthorne find both good and evil on both sides? Does he take a stand in favor of one group or the other?

Interaction

1. May Day celebrations in Western civilization go back to the Roman festival of Flora. They were common throughout English and European history. One attempt was made to perpetuate the May Day traditions in the New World in the colony at Mount Wollaston, Massachusetts, under the leadership of one Thomas Morton. Hawthorne based his story on the following account in Governor Bradford's journal:

And Morton became Lord of Misrule, and maintained (as it were) a School of Atheism. . . . They also set up a maypole, drinking and dancing about it many days together, inviting the Indian women for their consorts, dancing and frisking together like so many fairies, or furies, rather. As if they had anew revived and celebrated the feasts of the Roman goddess Flora, or the beastly practices of the mad Bacchanalians. Morton, likewise, to show his poetry composed sundry rhymes and verses, some tending to lasciviousness . . . which he affixed to this idle or idol maypole. They changed also the name of their place, and instead of calling it Mount Wollaston they called it

Merry Mount, as if this jollity would have lasted forever. But this continued not long, for . . . shortly after came the worthy gentleman Mr. John Endicott . . . who visiting these parts, caused that maypole to be cut down and rebuked them for their profaneness and admonished them to look there should be better walking.

Compare the events in Hawthorne's source material with the plot of "The Maypole of Merry Mount." What does Hawthorne add to Bradford's account? What does he omit? How is his attitude toward the conflict different from that of Bradford?

2. Defend John Endicott's actions at Merry Mount. Show, from Endicott's point of view, why the May celebrations had to be eliminated; why the maypole had to be cut down; why he punished the revelers; and why he placed the garland of flowers on the heads of the young lovers. You may wish to write an essay in the form of a first-person narrative with Endicott as speaker.

3. In one of Hawthorne's early stories, "The New Adam and Eve," Adam observes, "And now we must . . . try to discover what sort of world this is and why we have been sent hither." Many critics have interpreted Merry Mount as a garden of Eden. In this reading, Edgar and Edith become an American Adam and Eve who lose their innocence and learn the real meaning and responsibilities of life.

Discuss the fall of the colony at Merry Mount and the fate of the young lovers. What sort of world will they discover when they leave Merry Mount? What has been lost? What has been gained?

Young Goodman Brown

Text pages 198–210

Study Guide

1. Early in the story, Hawthorne says that Young Goodman Brown is setting out for an "evil purpose." His journey is presented as mysterious and ominous. What are some of the words and phrases in the opening paragraphs that create this atmosphere?

2. When does the reader know for certain that the old man is the devil? What symbolism do you find in the old man's staff? Whom does the old man resemble?

3. Why does Goodman Brown hesitate along the path? What finally makes him decide to go through with his "evil purpose" and attend the midnight meeting? What effect does the pink ribbon have upon him?
4. What does he find out about his own ancestors? about the "good" people of Salem, such as Goody Cloyse, the minister, and Deacon Gookin?
5. List the details about the midnight ceremony of evil which are similar to authentic religious ceremonies.
6. How did Brown feel when he saw that "the good shrank not from the wicked, nor were the sinners abashed by the saints"? What is the meaning of the leader's words: "Welcome, my children, to the communion of your race"?
7. Hawthorne has left the end of Goodman Brown's forest journey deliberately mysterious: neither Brown himself nor the reader knows for certain whether the midnight ceremony took place or whether it was a dream. What did Goodman Brown actually find when he returned to Salem? What new knowledge did he have? How did his knowledge change him?
8. **Symbol.** As always, Hawthorne writes in terms of symbols. Two examples are the names of the leading characters: *Goodman Brown* and *Faith*. Do they represent the qualities we usually associate with their names? Comment on Brown's saying to the devil: "Faith kept me back a while." What other symbols do you see in the story?

Interaction

1. Do you agree or disagree with the following statements about Hawthorne and "Young Goodman Brown"? Discuss each with specific reference to the story.
    a) The story suggests that it is impossible for us to know the ultimate good and evil in another person's heart — even those closest to us.
    b) After his dream or vision Goodman Brown is guilty of the sin of Despair. He has lost his faith in the possibility of goodness, and sets himself apart from the rest of humanity.
    c) Although the story is set in Salem around the year 1690, its meaning holds true for any town or city at any time.
2. Herman Melville, the author of *Moby Dick* and Hawthorne's friend, reviewed *Twice-Told Tales*, the book of short stories in which "Young Goodman Brown" originally appeared. In a phrase

that has become famous he said that Hawthorne was gifted with "the power of blackness," a power that came from a sense of man's "Innate Depravity and Original Sin." He went on to say that in certain moods no deeply thinking man "can weigh this world without throwing in something, somehow like Original Sin, to strike the uneven balance." How did "the power of blackness" affect Goodman Brown's life?
3. Hawthorne refuses to say whether or not Brown's vision was "true" or only a dream. In your opinion should Hawthorne have answered the question?

---

from Hawthorne's Notebooks

Text page 211

How does an author compose? Where does he get his ideas? How does his own experience of life become literature?

Some writers, like Mark Twain and Ernest Hemingway, travel widely and lead adventurous lives which feed their imaginations. Others, like Emily Dickinson, who hardly ever left her house in Amherst, Massachusetts, find the sources of their work within themselves. Though Hawthorne traveled in Europe after he had become a successful writer, the early years of his life — when he was writing "The Maypole of Merry Mount" and "Young Goodman Brown" — were spent very close to his home. In a famous entry in his *Notebooks*, dated *Salem, Union Street, October 25, 1836*, Hawthorne tells us, "In this dismal chamber FAME was won."

Hawthorne's *Notebooks* were an important source for his fiction. In them he kept a record of his travels, friendships, and his observations of the world. He became a collector of human experience, jotting down his thoughts on human nature and ideas that came to him for stories and novels. "Think nothing too trifling to write down," he advised, "so long as it be in the smallest degree characteristic. You will be surprised to find, on reperusing your journal, what an importance and graphic power these little particulars assume."

Interaction

1. What examples do you find in the entries of "little particulars" taking on more than a literal meaning?

2. Discuss the entry beginning "The human heart to be allegorized as a cavern . . ." in relation to "Young Goodman Brown." Was Goodman Brown able to go deeper than the stage of bewilderment and "terrible gloom"? Explain.
3. Select one of the following entries from Hawthorne's *Notebooks*, and expand it into a brief sketch or story:
   a) A sketch to be given of a modern reformer. . . . He goes about the streets haranguing most eloquently, and is on the point of making many converts, when his labors are suddenly interrupted by the appearance of the keeper of a madhouse, whence he has escaped. Much may be made of this idea.
   b) Cannon transformed to church bells.
   c) The scene of a story or sketch to be laid within the light of a street-lantern; the time, when the lamp is near going out; and the catastrophe to be simultaneous with the last flickering gleam.
   d) A tree tall and venerable to be said by tradition to have been the staff of some famous man who happened to thrust it into the ground, where it took root.

Ritual and Myth

The Lottery

Text pages 216–224

SHIRLEY JACKSON 1919–1965

"The Lottery" was the first of Shirley Jackson's explorations into the darker recesses of the human consciousness. The story raised a furor in 1948 when it first appeared in the *New Yorker;* many readers found it puzzling and even offensive. Shirley Jackson later wrote *We Have Always Lived in the Castle* and *The Haunting of Hill House.* Another and lighter side of Miss Jackson appears in *Life Among the Savages,* a collection of personal sketches about her family life in rural Vermont with her husband and four children.

THE SCAPEGOAT RITUAL

Shirley Jackson refused to discuss "The Lottery" for many years. Finally, twelve years after its publication, she remarked that the inspiration for the story came to her while she was on her way to the market. Nothing could be further from this peaceful, ordinary ritual than the scapegoat ritual, the ceremony in which a person or an animal takes the responsibility for everyone's guilt.

The word *scapegoat* comes from an ancient ceremony described in the Bible. According to the Old Testament (Leviticus 16), the priest put his hands on the head of a live goat and confessed the wrongs of his people. A demon, or *scape,* was believed to be transferred from the community to the goat, which was then driven into the wilderness.

Sir James Frazer, in his famous work *The Golden Bough,* reports scapegoat rituals in primitive cultures the world over. A western Himalayan tribe, for instance, once a year would chase a dog from their village and kill it with sticks and stones to protect the town from misfortune. Certain Solomon Islanders would annually drive a dog, supposedly bearing their diseases, over a cliff into the sea.

There have been human scapegoats as well. In one African community sinners used to contribute money during the year for the purchase of sickly individuals who were put to death to atone for the wrongs of the entire town.

The ancient Greeks, whose civilization we praise, had human scapegoats too. The Athenians at one time kept a number of social outcasts at public expense to be sacrificed during periods of plague or famine — one for the men and one for the women. The victims were paraded about the city and stoned to death outside its walls.

These rituals were thought to purchase the favor of the gods among people who associated misfortune — such as a poor harvest — with sin and guilt. Note that in "The Lottery" Old Man Warner repeats one of the community's ancient sayings, "Lottery in June, corn be heavy soon."

The scapegoat ritual and the myths behind it seem to be rooted in human psychology. When people feel guilty, they may wish to punish themselves. Just as often the punishment is taken out on someone or something else. That is why today we've come to think of a scapegoat as an innocent person who is unjustly blamed for a bad situation.

Study Guide

1. **Setting.** The characters in "The Lottery" have common American names: Bobby and Harry Jones, Mr. Summers, Tessie Hutchinson, and Joe Dunbar are just a few examples. The characters also talk about "planting and rain, tractors and taxes." (page 217) Where and when does the story take place? How does the setting contribute to the impact of the ending?

2. **Character.** The writer and critic E. M. Forster has distinguished between *flat* and *round* characters. *Flat* characters are painted for us in broad outline; we know just a few important things about them. *Round* characters are painted in detail; we know what they are thinking and feeling. Are the characters in "The Lottery" flat or round? How does Shirley Jackson make them seem like typical, ordinary people?

3. What parts of the lottery ritual have been changed or lost? What remains? The people do not seem to understand why the lottery originally began. Why, then, do you think they continue to observe it every year?

4. Many of the people feel nervous about the lottery before the lots are drawn. Tessie, however, seems to be in a good humor. How does Tessie's attitude change after her family is chosen? How do the rest of the people feel when they themselves are no longer in any danger? What human traits do these shifts in attitude bring out?
5. Before Tessie is chosen, the following things happen:
    a) The townspeople worry that Mrs. Dunbar won't have a man to draw for her family.
    b) Everyone praises young Jack Watson for drawing for his family.
    c) The people are neighborly and greet each other with small jokes.
    d) Someone helps little Davy draw.
    e) Mr. Summers takes time to explain the drawing to Davy.
    What do these events tell us about the townspeople? Why is the ending a shock?
6. When did you first become aware that events were taking a sinister turn? What effect does Miss Jackson achieve by withholding the shocking nature of the ritual? Briefly look again at the story. What early clues do you discover concerning the story's outcome?

Interaction

1. What does the lottery in the story have in common with scapegoat rituals? What do you think Shirley Jackson says about rituals in this story? What do you think she says about the capabilities of nice, ordinary people?
2. "The Lottery" takes an ancient primitive ritual and places it in a modern setting. But American communities do not literally stone people as part of a ritual. In what sense, then, do civilized communities use people as scapegoats?
    Look again for a moment at the opening of "The Outcasts of Poker Flat." (pages 44–45) How are the outcasts used as scapegoats? Can you think of any examples of present-day scapegoats?
3. Some readers accused Shirley Jackson of writing the story as a clever hoax. Others thought it was a great work of art. Some felt it makes twisted and ugly observations about human nature. Others felt it makes profound and true comments about human nature. What do you think of this story? What does it have in common with "The Maypole of Merry Mount"?

Perseus

Text page 225

Robert Hayden   *born:* 1913

Robert Hayden is a professor of English and a poet. Much of his poetry reflects his interest in Negro history and folklore. He has also written poems based on his boyhood in Detroit. He wrote "Perseus" after seeing an artist's interpretation of the myth in a museum.

Study Guide

1. In this poem Perseus is the speaker. The first stanza tells us what thought flashed through his mind just before he slew Medusa. The second stanza tells us how he felt afterward. What urge was aroused in Perseus by the slaying?
2. In the first stanza Perseus says that Medusa's face reflected in his shield reminded him of "hated truth the mind accepts at last and festers on." What "hated truth" does Perseus come to recognize? What is Hayden saying happens to a person who commits a violent act?

To Helen

Text page 226

Edgar Allan Poe   (biography pages 75–76)

This poem is rich in classical allusions — references to the legends of ancient Greece and Rome. A summary of these allusions is given below to help you understand the poem:
   a) *Helen:* the beautiful Greek queen who was carried off to Troy by Paris, thus causing the Trojan War. She is a symbol of womanly beauty.
   b) *Nicéan:* a reference to an ancient seafaring people.
   c) *hyacinth hair:* curly, like the blossoms of the hyacinth.
   d) *Naiad airs:* the songs of water nymphs.
   e) *Psyche:* the girl who married Cupid, the god of love. She is the personification of the soul.

Study Guide

1. "To Helen" is very different from the usual love poem or love song. One reason for this difference is that Poe is not just talking about a woman; he is talking about an ideal of womanhood. The love he describes is not the passion of the "moon–June–spoon" lyric; it is perfect or ideal love. How do the allusions help create a picture of ideal womanhood and ideal love?
2. In the first stanza the speaker says that Helen's beauty is like a ship that brings a "weary, way-worn wanderer" home. This comparison may seem puzzling at first. Consider the action described in the stanza as a metaphor for the speaker's feelings. What does the phrase "weary, way-worn wanderer" tell us about his feelings? How does Helen's beauty change these feelings?
3. In the second stanza, the speaker describes Helen as the ideal of physical beauty. Then, in the third stanza, he pictures her enveloped in light; he addresses her as Psyche and thinks of her as a being from a "Holy Land." What kind of beauty in Helen does he describe in this last stanza?
4. In each stanza the speaker is "brought" to a different place: in stanza one, "his own native shore"; in stanza two, "the glory that was Greece,/And the grandeur that was Rome"; in stanza three, "Holy Land." These are the places the speaker seems to have been searching for as he roamed the "desperate seas." How is each place more ideal than the one before?

Phaethon

Text page 227

Morris Bishop   (biography page 34)

Study Guide

1. "Phaethon" is a poem which appears to be one thing and turns out to be another. What surprises do the last two lines reveal?

2. Even before we reach the last two lines, we can see that this is not a serious treatment of the myth. What colloquial expressions set the humorous tone? Read the poem aloud to discover the comic rhymes which set the humorous tone.

Interaction

1. The word *myth* is used in many ways and has several different meanings. Look up *myth* in a good unabridged dictionary. Which definitions best apply to each of the following uses of the word?
   a) the myth of the frontier
   b) the myth that thunder results when Henry Hudson's men are bowling
   c) the myth that good always wins out in the end
   d) the myth of Perseus
2. We no longer "believe" in the Greek myths. Nor do we practice such primitive rituals as scapegoat ceremonies. Why, then, do you think that modern writers continue to draw upon ancient myths and rituals as a source for their writing?

The Bible

Meditation Six

Text page 228

EDWARD TAYLOR   1645–1729

Edward Taylor emigrated from England to Boston in 1668. After graduation from Harvard, he became the doctor and pastor in Westfield, Massachusetts, then a frontier town. Although he was a Puritan and followed the Puritan traditions of austerity and simplicity, Taylor wrote his sacred poetry in a highly ornate and intellectual style.

Poets of seventeenth-century England and America often wrote about religious experience in terms of everyday things — coins, purses, and spectacles, for example. They also liked to use a single item as a metaphor that extended throughout the poem. This is what Edward Taylor does in "Meditation Six." The Angel is the metaphor around which he organizes his poem.

The word *angel* has a double meaning: (1) a spiritual being and (2) a coin. Many puns and double meanings appear in this poem. Although today we tend to associate puns with humorous writing, poets in Taylor's time used them seriously. But before going on to a close look at them, read the poem as a prayer. What do you think Edward Taylor is praying for?

Study Guide

1. What question does Taylor ask God in the first stanza?
2. At least four puns appear in stanza one:
   a) *count*: (1) to be included (2) to judge (3) to add up
   b) *o'er*: the contraction of *over*, sounds like *ore*
   c) *touchstone*: (1) a stone used to test the quality of gold; a poor quality discolors or "touches" (2) a high standard
   d) *try*: (1) to test (2) to put a heavy strain on
   In what way is Taylor like a gold coin? What fear does he express in this stanza?
3. In stanzas two and three, several things connected with minting coins are mentioned: stamp, image, inscription, plate, superscription. In what way is the speaker like a coin being minted?
4. By the time we reach the end of the poem, we can see that the last two lines suggest many things. What are some of the things these lines suggest to you?

The Creation

Text pages 229–231

James Weldon Johnson 1871–1938

James Weldon Johnson's remarkable life story includes successes as a teacher, high school principal, attorney, diplomat, songwriter, and poet. Early in his career he expanded the curriculum of the Negro school in his Florida home town to include the high school grades. He was the first Negro attorney admitted to the Florida bar since the Civil War. And he was U.S. Consul in Venezuela and Nicaragua and secretary of the NAACP.

His career as a writer began in 1910 with *The Autobiography of an Ex-Colored Man*. He then began writing poetry, including *God's Trombones* and *Black Manhattan*.

Study Guide

1. One reader of this poem felt that it expresses the idea that "God created man in his own image, and man created God in his own image." How does the preacher in James Weldon Johnson's poem "humanize" God?
2. In this poem God is seen literally as the Maker. That is, he creates the physical universe in the same way that a man might fashion a work of art. What are some of the images of muscular movement used to show the creation?

Interaction

1. The opening verses of the first chapter of Genesis begin with these words:

> In the beginning God created the heaven and the earth.
> And the earth was without form, and void; and darkness was upon the face of the deep. And the Spirit of God moved upon the face of the waters.
> And God said, Let there be light: and there was light.
> And God saw the light, that it was good: and God divided the light from the darkness.
> And God call the light Day, and the darkness he called Night. And the evening and the morning were the first day.
> And God said, Let there be a firmament in the midst of the waters, and let it divide the waters from the waters.
> And God made the firmament, and divided the waters which were under the firmament from the waters which were above the firmament: and it was so.
> And God called the firmament Heaven. And the evening and the morning were the second day.
> And God said, Let the waters under the heaven be gathered together unto one place, and let the dry land appear: and it was so.
> And God called the dry land Earth; and the gathering together of the waters called he Seas: and God saw that it was good.

How does the preacher in Johnson's poem reinterpret these lines for his congregation? What biblical expressions are retained?
2. Compare "Meditation Six" and "The Creation." What is different about the way each poet pictures God and religion? How does each poet relate religious experience to everyday life?
3. Taylor's poem is a *meditation*, a private prayer. Johnson's poem, on the other hand, is a sermon and therefore attuned to spoken language. With your classmates, plan a choral reading of "The Creation." Assign parts and make up voice directions. Select music that you feel would be fitting as a background to the choral reading.

from Conquistadors in North American History

Text pages 234–242

PAUL HORGAN   born: 1903

Paul Horgan spent many years in the Southwest as librarian of the New Mexico Military Institute at Roswell. His historical studies, particularly of the Southwest, are known for being "excellently researched and eminently readable" and for giving "more of the Indian viewpoint than is usually found." Among his many books are *Peter Hurd: A Portrait* and *A Distant Trumpet*.

Study Guide

1. Even in ancient times, it was customary for generals to hire a historian, or chronicler, to travel with the army and record important events. The Spanish chronicler whom Horgan uses as one source for *Conquistadors* was Cortés's historian. What kind of information does Horgan rely on the Spanish chronicler for? Why would a historian like Horgan have to use other sources as well, and not rely entirely upon the Spanish chronicler?

2. When Paul Horgan wrote *Conquistadors in North American History,* he did more than simply catalogue dates, battles, and treaties. He included gossip, strange and surprising portraits, the conflicts and attitudes of the people who made history, and even his own humorous view of certain things, for example: "The soldiers found themselves becoming fond of him . . . despite treason and idolatry and a taste for stewed boy." (page 236) What incidents, attitudes, and details add excitement to history in this selection?

3. What were some of the conflicts between the Spanish and the Mexican cultures?

4. Montezuma was sometimes the enemy, sometimes the friend of the Spaniards. How did Cortés and his men react to the news of Montezuma's death? What are some of the things Horgan brings out about Cortés as a man and as a general?

5. The bare facts of the Mexican conquest are that the Spaniards were foreign invaders (*imperialists* might be the word today) while the Mexicans were defending their homeland. It would be easy for a historian to slant his history in favor of the underdog or to romanticize the conquerors. Does Horgan slant his history in favor of one group or the other? Where does he show sympathy for the Mexicans? for the Spaniards?

from John Brown's Body

Text pages 243–260

STEPHEN VINCENT BENÉT   1898–1943

Stephen Vincent Benét was born to a military family and grew up on army bases around the country. His father, grandfather, and great-grandfather were army officers, and as a boy Benét pored over military records they had collected. He hoped someday to base a long narrative poem on these records. Years later, after achieving success as a novelist and short-story writer, Benét wrote the patriotic epic *John Brown's Body*, based on the family records and his own minute knowledge of the Civil War years. The long poem, one of the most widely read poems of the late twenties and early thirties, won for Benét a Pulitzer Prize. It also won him the reputation of the national poet-historian. The poet Harriet Monroe called *John Brown's Body* a "cinema epic," and it is considered Benét's greatest work. He is also known for *The Devil and Daniel Webster*, which has become a classic American short story.

Study Guide

JOHN BROWN

1. The brief introduction in the anthology (page 243) indicates that there were many sides to John Brown, both good and bad. What does Benét bring out about John Brown's behavior during his last month? Does Benét give a balanced picture of Brown, or is the portrait totally sympathetic?

2. Northerners who did not actually participate in the raid had backed it. How did they react when Brown was captured? (lines 4–14) Benét writes that the North had "now begun/To mold his body into crucified Christ's." How did Brown feel about being turned into a martyr? How does Benét emphasize Brown the man rather than Brown the martyr?
3. *John Brown's Body* is history related by a poet. Where does Benét see events with the poet's eye rather than the historian's?

LINCOLN

1. The opening description of Lincoln is the portrait of a man, not a legend or an ossified historical figure. What are some of the homey and humanizing details Benét includes?
2. Beginning with line 37, Benét makes use of the poet's privilege and writes from Lincoln's point of view. Lincoln's thoughts are often phrased in homespun language; for example: "The Union's too big a horse to keep changing the saddle." (line 46) What other homespun similes and metaphors does Benét use? What does this language tell us about Lincoln?
3. What are some of the thoughts that go through Lincoln's mind? What decision does he have to make at that moment?

GRANT

1. Benét compares Grant with Napoleon and Caesar in the first lines. What are some of the things the three have in common?
2. Why was Grant "unlikely material"?
3. Lines 24–30 give a factual account of Grant's response to Lincoln's call to arms. What is ironic about these facts?
4. Both John Brown and Lincoln are portrayed sympathetically. Could it be said that Grant is portrayed as a *pathetic* figure? Why or why not?

LEE

1. In the opening lines Benét writes that Lee is "Frozen into a legend out of life." (line 27) How do the opening and closing lines give us a sense of the heroic, legendary, "marble" Lee?
2. Certain ancient Greek philosophers believed that proportion — moderation in all things — was the highest virtue. Benét writes that Lee was a model of "Greek proportion." In what ways was Lee a model of this Greek ideal?

3. This "Greek proportion" seems to Benét to make Lee "a riddle unread." Benét wants to "humanize" Lee, to get beyond "All the sick honey of the speechifiers." (line 33) Why is this so difficult? Do you think that Benét has humanized Lee?
4. In his portrait of Lee, Benét includes only one quotation from Lee's actual words: "I'm always wanting something." (page 253) What does Benét find significant in these words?

GETTYSBURG — PICKETT'S CHARGE

1. Benét describes the young George Pickett as ". . . a boy who dreamt of a martial sword . . . in the old bright way of the tales." (lines 16–18) In what way was the charge a fulfillment of these dreams? In what ways was the reality totally unlike the dreams?
2. Benét stresses action rather than character in this segment of the poem. What actions illustrate the heroism of both armies?
3. The language of this segment contains a great many images and comparisons. For example, Benét continually compares the charging soldiers to a tide. (lines 28, 36, 44) What other images and comparisons do you notice?

THE END OF THE WAR

1. In what way does this segment draw together many of the strands of the previous segments?
2. After the meeting between the two commanding generals, there are many different immediate reactions. What are the different reactions of General Lee, the men in the room where the peace was concluded, and the blue and gray armies outside the farmhouse?
3. When Benét writes "It is over, now . . . ," the tone is solemn rather than joyful. How do the opening lines, showing Lincoln in Richmond, emphasize the tragedy of the war? How do the final lines emphasize a sense of loss rather than a feeling of triumph and joy?

Interaction

1. Historian Bruce Catton writes, "Grant and Lee were in complete contrast, representing two diametrically opposed elements in

American life." Contrast Grant and Lee as Benét portrays them. How do the two generals contrast at the meeting at Appomattox? (page 259)

2. Benét based his work on research, just as a historian would. Yet *John Brown's Body* is a poem, not a work of history. What does Benét add to the facts that a historian would not? In what way is Benét more selective? What different purposes and responsibilities would a poet have in contrast to a historian?

3. One of the remarkable qualities of *John Brown's Body* is its form. Because he does not limit himself to one particular rhythm or rhyme scheme, Benét is able to suit the rhythm of each segment to its subject and mood. His language, too, is dictated by his subject. For example, consider the differences in rhythm and language between "John Brown" (page 243) and "Gettysburg — Pickett's Charge." (page 255) Consider also the contrast between "Lincoln" (page 246) and "Lee." (page 250) Reading lines from each segment aloud will help you hear the differences in the rhythm and diction. What are some of these differences?

The Civil War: Three Memorial Poems

Shiloh

Text page 261

Herman Melville 1819–1891

Just before his twentieth birthday, Herman Melville left his home in Albany, New York, and went to sea. He traveled over most of the globe on merchant ships, men-of-war, and whaling ships. He was involved in a mutiny and marooned on a tropical island. He witnessed the white man's cruelty to the primitive peoples who welcomed him, and he observed the brutality of life on board ship.

When Melville returned to Albany it was to find out what kind of a man his travels had made him — to learn more about himself by writing. "From my twenty-fifth year," he told Nathaniel Hawthorne, "I date my life." For a while he could write simply as a man of action relating adventures at sea, and he became famous, at the age of twenty-seven, as the author of *Typee: A Peep at Polynesian Life* and *Omoo: A Narrative of Adventures in the South Seas*. But Melville soon became dissatisfied with his reputation as "the man who lived among cannibals," and he never again wrote to please his critics and readers. "What I feel most moved to write" he confided to Hawthorne, "that is banned — it will not pay. Yet, altogether, write the *other* way I cannot."

In 1851 Melville finished his masterpiece. *Moby Dick* was not just an adventure story about the pursuit of the Leviathan — the legendary white whale; it was the pursuit of belief, and a struggle against the conditions that govern a man's life. In this book, as in all his best writing, Melville sought the principles of good and evil which govern the universe.

By 1866 Melville was earning so little as a writer that, like Hawthorne before him, he went to work in a customhouse. The four volumes of poetry that he composed during these twenty years of drudgery are becoming increasingly well known and respected. During the last three years before his death in 1891 Melville wrote one other great piece of fiction, *Billy Budd*, which was not published until thirty-nine years after his death.

Nathaniel Hawthorne was the only writer of the period who recognized Melville's greatness. "He can neither believe nor be comfortable in his unbelief," Hawthorne wrote in his *Notebooks*, "and he is too honest and courageous not to try to do one or the other. If he were a religious man he would be one of the most truly religious and reverential; he has a very high and noble nature, and better worth immortality than most of us." Today Melville is recognized as one of the greatest writers America has produced.

Study Guide

1. How does the natural landscape contrast with the events at Shiloh?
2. In what sense are the soldiers "Foemen at morn, but friends at eve — "?
3. Melville writes ironically, "What like a bullet can undeceive!" What does he feel the soldiers had been "deceived" about?
4. A *requiem* is a hymn for the dead. In this requiem Melville neither praises the dead nor commemorates the victory. What seems to you to be the purpose of the poem?

Ode

Text page 262

Henry Timrod   1828–1867

Henry Timrod was born in South Carolina, and his poems on his native South won him the name of Laureate of the Confederacy. Poor health forced Timrod to leave the army after a year of service during the Civil War. He then returned to poetry and edited a newspaper, which was destroyed during Sherman's march. Timrod's most famous poem is this "Ode," or lyric to the Confederate dead.

Study Guide

1. Stephen Vincent Benét describes Confederate commander George Pickett as a soldier who idealized war "in the old bright way of the tales." Do you think Timrod idealizes the war dead? What is his purpose in this poem?
2. An ode is a lyric poem often written in lofty language. Which of Timrod's expressions in this "Ode" might be considered "lofty"? Are they effective?

Memorial Wreath

Text page 263

Dudley Randall   *born:* 1914

Dudley Randall heads the Broadside Press, publishers of poems printed on beautifully decorated broadsides, which are large sheets of paper. He is also the translator of many modern Russian poets.

Study Guide

1. Unlike "Shiloh," "Memorial Wreath" does not re-create "the parched ones stretched in pain" or "many a parting groan." Instead Randall uses images that suggest life, blossoming, and vitality. What are some of these images? Why does he use these rather than images of death?

2. Randall alludes to Lincoln, Brown (John Brown), Douglass, and Toussaint. Why are these figures significant?
3. Henry Timrod calls the Confederate dead "martyrs." (line 2) Where does Randall indicate that the Negro dead were martyrs?

Interaction

1. The introduction to the "Ode" in the anthology (page 262) says that Timrod's poem could "readily serve as a tribute to the Northern dead as well." Do you agree? Explain why or why not.
2. "Shiloh" commemorates an event that took place in 1862. Timrod's "Ode" was written for a memorial ceremony held in 1867. And Randall's "Memorial Wreath" was published one hundred years after the Battle of Shiloh, in 1962. What attitude toward war — specifically, men dying for a cause — underlies each poem? Which poem do you think best expresses the attitudes of people today?

DARK VOICES IN AMERICAN LITERATURE

Although Hawthorne often criticized the stiffness and gloom of the Puritans, he did inherit from them something that many American writers share: a fascination with the dark side of human nature. In his novels and tales, Hawthorne explored "the Unpardonable Sin," which he described in his *Notebooks:*

> The Unpardonable Sin might consist in a want of love and reverence for the Human Soul; in consequence of which, the investigator pried into its dark depths, not with a hope or purpose of making it better, but from a cold philosophical curiosity. . . . Would not this, in other words, be the separation of the intellect from the heart?
>
> The search of an investigator for the Unpardonable Sin; — he at last finds it in his own heart and practice.

In the selections in this unit you will see variations on this theme, beginning with the Puritan minister Thomas Hooker, who analyzed sin in order to achieve a "true sight" (or insight into) evil.

Two Puritan Sermons

A True Sight of Sin

Text pages 267–268

THOMAS HOOKER 1586–1647

Thomas Hooker was a Puritan who fled England in 1630 and, after three years in Holland, embarked for New England. He became the pastor of a church in what is now Cambridge, Massachusetts. Three years later he led a group from his parish one hundred miles south to found Hartford in the valley of the Connecticut River. Hooker's leadership in this new democratic community was dynamic, and he is considered the first great American preacher.

Study Guide

1. According to Hooker, why should men "see clearly the nature of sin in his naked hue"? (page 267)

2. Explain Hooker's reasons for making the following statements (page 268):
   a) "Sin deprives me of my greatest good for which I came into the world. . . ."
   b) ". . . sin is the greatest evil in the world."
   c) ". . . it's better to suffer all plagues without any one sin than to commit the least sin and to be freed from all plagues."
3. What warning or threat is implied in the final sentence? What response do you think Hooker desired from his congregation?

Interaction

1. What signs do you see that Edward Taylor (page 228) and Thomas Hooker shared the same religion? Does one's image of God differ from the other's? Which selection is more personal? Which is the more impersonal?
2. Recall Hawthorne's definition of the Unpardonable Sin: ". . . a want of love and reverence for the Human Soul; . . . the separation of the intellect from the heart." Is Hawthorne's conception of sin essentially similar to or different from Hooker's? Explain your answer.

---

from Sinners in the Hands of an Angry God

Text pages 269–271

JONATHAN EDWARDS   (biography text page 269)

Study Guide

1. To dramatize the principles of his faith, Edwards uses an image which has since become famous: "The God that holds you over the pit of hell, much as one holds a spider or some loathsome insect over the fire. . . ." (page 270) How does Edwards complete this passage? What idea of the relation of man to God does this image reveal?
2. The entire sermon continues for five more pages, documenting the fierceness of God's wrath, and ending with a call to renounce vanity and accept Christ. In general, Edwards uses metaphor

sparingly, but paragraphs 1, 2, and 5 contain three extended metaphors. Explain each metaphor and give reasons why you think they make the passage more, or less, effective.

3. According to Edwards, why have the sinners in his church not already been destroyed?

4. Why would he choose to present his views in such dramatic language? What response might he have desired from the members of his congregation?

5. Does Edwards say that *all* men are sinners? What hope of salvation does he hold out? (See paragraph 3.)

Interaction

1. Compare Edwards's attitude toward sin and guilt with the attitudes of the Puritans in Hawthorne's "The Maypole of Merry Mount." How might Hawthorne have reacted to the sermon?

2. Compare the Puritan sermon by Hooker (page 267) to Edwards's sermon. What are the differences in tone? in style? in the kind of logic employed?

3. Jonathan Edwards read with dignity and restraint. But according to one member of his congregation, "There was such a breathing of distress and weeping" when the sermon was delivered, that "the preacher was obliged to speak to the people and desire silence, that he might be heard."

   Imagine you are a member of the original congregation. Would your response be "distress and weeping"? As a twentieth-century reader, how do you respond? What changes account for the differences?

4. As an exercise, try delivering this sermon aloud. What should the speaker do to make his delivery effective? Are there any advantages to hearing and speaking the sermon instead of reading it silently? If so, what are they?

5. An interesting project for the entire class (or a committee of at least six members belonging to different churches) is to ask a number of ministers, priests, and rabbis to read and comment on this passage. Then report to the class on the attitudes of modern clergymen toward this style of preaching and toward the ideas expressed.

The Fall of the House of Usher

Text pages 272–290

Edgar Allan Poe 1809–1849

Edgar Allan Poe was the first American master of the tale of horror and suspense, but he was something more besides. In his short life of poverty and tragedy he developed a theory of literature that led to the recognition of the short story as a new and important form of writing. His poems and his ideas about poetry had a deep influence on European writers and, through them, on American poets of the twentieth century. With some of his stories, like "The Murders in the Rue Morgue," he originated the detective story. Stories like "A Descent into the Maelstrom" make him the forerunner of the modern science-fiction writer. But more important, he established a new kind of fiction — one which uses symbols and psychological analysis to explore the darker side of man's inner life. Some of the stories, such as "The Cask of Amontillado" and "The Pit and the Pendulum," explore the minds of criminals and madmen. Poe became what the English novelist D. H. Lawrence called "an adventurer into the vaults and cellars and horrible underground passages of the human soul." Many of his most characteristic works, such as "Ligeia," "The Raven," or "The Fall of the House of Usher," show a solitary man, torn in spirit, searching for a lost ideal, a vision of perfect beauty, or an unattainable goal. And though he never wrote directly about his own experiences, the story of Poe's inner life was very similar.

The son of traveling actors, Edgar Poe was born in Boston in 1809. He was orphaned before the age of three by his father's desertion and the death of his mother. A wealthy couple in Richmond, Virginia, Mr. and Mrs. John Allan, gave him the education and upbringing of a young Virginia gentleman. Poe later added the Allans' name to his own, but, after a series of violent quarrels with his guardians, he left Richmond at the age of eighteen. He worked his way north to Boston under one alias, and enlisted in the army under another. In the meantime he had written his first volume of poetry, signed only "a Bostonian." After two years as a soldier — and the publication of his second book of poems — Poe was admitted to West Point. But when it became clear that he could expect no inheritance from his guardian, Poe left the military life with no real hope of finding a suitable place for himself in society. "My future life must be passed in indigence and sickness," he wrote at this time, and the prophecy proved correct.

For a while he lived and worked in Baltimore, producing there in 1831 a third book of poems, which showed increased skill. Now that he was dependent on his writing for his livelihood he turned to prose. He won a literary contest in 1833 for his short story "MS Found in a Bottle," but the prize money for such stories was not enough to live on. Poe became an editor for the *Southern Literary Review*, the first of similar positions with literary magazines he was to hold in New York and Philadelphia. Poe was hardworking and successful as an editor. He found and encouraged the best literary talent of his day. As a critic, he reviewed works by Hawthorne, Henry Wadsworth Longfellow, and James Russell Lowell; he was feared and respected for his dedication and integrity. Only the inner violence and conflict in his temperament prevented him from settling down with his young wife, Virginia, and disproving his own prophecy.

As an author — and this was the most important of Poe's careers — he was still unrecognized and unrewarded. A collection of short stories, *Tales of the Arabesque and Grotesque*, was published in 1840, but only under the condition that the publisher receive the profits. Though he was working with increasing sureness and artistry, Poe's personal life became more hectic and disrupted, particularly by the thoughts of his wife's illness and approaching death. In 1845 his major volume of poetry, which included "The Raven," brought him widespread recognition, and a year later he gained control of his own magazine — a goal he had pursued unsuccessfully for years. "My life has been *whim* — impulse — passion — " he wrote at this time, "a longing for solitude, a scorn of all things present in an earnest longing for the future." But during the next year his wife died. Shortly afterward, Poe's magazine failed for lack of funds. The rest of his life, even though he was publishing some of his most successful work, was a story of poverty, illness, mistaken love, and frequent periods of depression and instability. "The truth is," he admitted, "I am heartily sick of this life and of the nineteenth century in general; I am convinced that everything is going wrong." In the summer of 1849, hoping to begin a new magazine, Poe returned to Richmond where he met and became engaged to a childhood sweetheart, now a wealthy widow. After starting north in September to attend to some unfinished business, he was found unconscious in Baltimore. Poe died four days later at the age of forty.

Comment

Since the days of the alchemists no one has produced more than Poe the effects of damnation, no one has been more conscious of being damned. In his pages the breath of life never stirs: crimes occur which do not reverberate in the human conscience, there is laughter which has no sound, there is weeping without tears, there is beauty without love, there is love without children, trees grow which bear no fruit, flowers which have no fragrance — it is a silent world, cold, blasted, moon-struck, sterile, a devil's heath. Only a sensation of intolerable remorse pervades it.

Poe is commonly called unreal; it is justly said of him that he never touches the general heart of man, that perhaps of all writers who have lived he has the least connection with human experience.

— VAN WYCK BROOKS: Our Poets

In his youth Poe tried to capture what he called "the sentiment of the beautiful — that divine sixth sense which is yet so faintly understood." However, later he became less concerned with beauty for its own sake. In a review of Nathaniel Hawthorne's *Twice-Told Tales*, Poe wrote that the good writer should combine only those events and emotions which produce a "single effect." "In the whole composition," according to Poe, "there should be no word written of which the tendency, direct or indirect, is not to the one preestablished design." It would seem that Poe wrote "The Fall of the House of Usher" so that every word, from the first sentence to the last, would intensify what he considered man's most basic emotion — "the grim phantasm, Fear."

For Poe, those matters which in real life could be clearly identified and accounted for in everyday terms had "a certain hardness" which "repels the artistic eye." Both complexity of detail and suggestiveness — an undercurrent of indefinite meaning — must be added. For this reason, Poe makes the Ushers's house itself a very mysterious and ambiguous place — a building which has a life and a power of its own and which sometimes merges with the lives of its inhabitants.

Study Guide

1. Why did the narrator come to the House of Usher? What are some of the features of the house and its landscape that "unnerved" him? What does he notice inside the house that adds to his fear and uncertainty? Do you see any interplay between the inner state of the narrator and his outer world? Explain.

2. Why did the phrase "the House of Usher" come to refer to "both the family and the family mansion"? Look at the description of the house on page 275. How does it foreshadow the fate of Roderick Usher? How do you interpret the physical decomposition of the house of Usher at the story's end? *It destroys as Usher falls*

3. What do we learn about Roderick Usher from his appearance, his choice of clothing, food, and books, his music, and his paintings? *Is aroused*

4. In light of the story's conclusion, what significance do you find in the subject of the one painting which is described in detail? (page 280) What are some of the ways in which "The Haunted Palace" resembles the house of Usher? What significant similarities do you see between the events in the *Mad Trist* and the conclusion to this story? (pages 286–288)

5. What does the narrator hear — besides the storm outside — as he reads from the *Mad Trist*? What do these sounds mean to Roderick Usher? Why? *The sister has come to destroy him. She was living when put in the tomb.*

6. What kind of person does the narrator seem to be? How is he affected by his visit with the Ushers? Do you see any hints that he, too, has gone mad? *He sees and feels what Usher feels. No*

7. What seems to be the role in the story of Roderick's twin sister, Lady Madeline? While in one sense we see Lady Madeline's death-embrace of her brother as revenge, in another sense it appears as a reunion of "soul companions" in death. Where in the story do you find grounds for such an interpretation?

Interaction

1. What are the "darker" aspects of human experience which Poe describes in "The Fall of the House of Usher"? What, if anything, does Poe share with Hooker and Taylor?

2. In planning a new novel, Hawthorne made this note: "The story must not be founded at all on remorse or secret guilt . . . all that Poe wore out." By "wore out" he meant that Poe had treated these subjects so often that they were exhausted. More than seventy-five years later, Van Wyck Brooks remarked about Poe: "perhaps of all writers who have lived he has the least connection with human experience."

   What is your opinion of "The Fall of the House of Usher"? Does it have little connection with human experience? That is, is it contrived just to be horrible? Or does it touch the profound human experiences of "remorse or secret guilt"?

Brother Carlyle

Text pages 291–294

WILLIAM MELVIN KELLEY *born:* 1937

William M. Kelley, born in New York City, studied at Harvard with poet-playwright Archibald MacLeish. Kelley's books, A *Different Drummer, Dancers on the Shore,* and A *Drop of Patience,* have brought him recognition as one of the most promising of young modern writers.

Study Guide

1. Although Carlyle is a youngster, Irene is afraid of him: "She spoke to him almost afraid, for this was not the first time he had done such things. . . ." (page 292) Why is his mother afraid of Carlyle? What happens when she tries to communicate her fears to her husband?
2. How do Mance and Mr. Bedlow feel about Carlyle? Does either one share Irene's fears?
3. Carlyle is a mysterious character. He smiles, nods, and says little. How does the father interpret Carlyle's behavior? Do you agree with his interpretation? What other interpretations might there be?
4. Look again at the last paragraph of the story, page 294. What future seems to be in store for each member of the Bedlow family?

Interaction

1. Although William Melvin Kelley's style differs from Poe's, both writers build a sense of fear in the reader. What fears does each writer portray? What darker side of human nature does each one look into?
2. Although Irene and her husband and children converse, their communication is stifled by fear and confusion. Discuss the ways in which the lack of communication affects family life, both in the story and your own experience.

The Little Stone Man

Text pages 295–306

OLIVER LA FARGE   1901–1963

Most of Oliver La Farge's stories and novels are about American Indians. An amateur archeologist and at one time president of the American Association on Indian Affairs, La Farge was a champion of the rights of Indians, both in his fiction and in various governmental offices.

Study Guide

1. What did the little figurine mean to the San Leandros? to the American anthropologists?
2. What foreshadowing of Charlie's betrayal of trust do you find in the early stages of the story? What led him to tell Dr. Sorenson what he did?
3. Charlie's report to the Professor caused the breakdown in his good relations with the San Leandro Indians. To what extent was Charlie's action a natural outcome of his trying to accept the ways of two different cultures?

Interaction

1. In a discussion of tragedy S. Leonard Rubinstein wrote:

   One concept of tragedy considers it the conflict of mutually exclusive goods, the conflict of good with good. To satisfy the requirements of one good, the requirements of the other good must be violated. An example is a man caught between wife and mother. Tragedy is no longer the conflict between good and evil, because their characters are no longer separable. The conflict then is between good and opposite good, of which the choice of either would violate the other. To choose neither would be to violate both.

   How was Charlie caught in a conflict between "good and opposite good"?
2. Most of the selections in this section, "Dark Voices in American Literature," explore a dark side of human nature. Oliver La Farge, however, seems to say less than Poe and Kelley about evil in mankind. Is anyone in the story evil? Is evil brought about intentionally or accidentally? If none of the individuals is evil, why

does evil arise from the situation? Through insensitivity? imprudence? the difficulty of total communication between the two cultures? the dead hand of tradition? Discuss each of these possibilities as well as others that occur to you.

The Portable Phonograph

Text pages 307–313

WALTER VAN TILBURG CLARK   *born:* 1909

Walter Clark grew up in Reno, Nevada, and has identified himself with the West in much of his writing. His West, however, is not a setting for high adventure, but for tragedy. His novel *The Ox-Bow Incident*, which has become a minor classic both as a book and as a film, deals with the lynching of three innocent men.

Study Guide

1. What details tell us that the story is set in the future? The first paragraph ends with "young trees trying again." How are the men in the story like these "young trees"?
2. The author does not introduce the four characters right away and when he does he refers to them as "the man who admired books," "the harsh man," and "the musician." Why do you suppose he did not name them?
3. Why do the circumstances of the story increase the men's regard for the arts? Where are the books and the phonograph treated as though they had religious significance?
4. The author's description of the performance of Debussy's nocturne (pages 311–312) is very detailed. Why is the musician's reaction to the music different from that of the other listeners?
5. On page 312 Clark writes, "In the rifts of clouds, the doctor saw four stars flying. It impressed the doctor that one of them had just been obscured by the beginning of a flying cloud. . . ." Whose death might this image foreshadow?
6. After the guests leave, Dr. Jenkins becomes very secretive, hiding his phonograph and books. He also arms himself with a lead pipe, as though he expects one of the guests to return to steal his phonograph. Is there any basis for the doctor's suspicion? Why

do you suppose he behaves this way? In other words, what attitudes have the men carried over to the "new" civilization? Look particularly at these lines on page 307: "A queer sensation of torment, of two-sided, unpredictable nature, arose from the stillness of the earth air beneath the violence of the upper air."

Interaction

Listen to a recording of one or all three of Debussy's nocturnes. Why is this music a good choice for the function it has in this story?

Ile

Text pages 314–329

EUGENE O'NEILL   1888–1953

Eugene O'Neill was the son of a famous romantic actor. As a youngster he traveled with his father's theatrical troupe, which performed such popular melodramas as *The Count of Monte Cristo*. After a year of college, he went to sea. He later recalled, "My ambition, if you could call it that, was to keep moving and do as many things as I could." O'Neill prospected for gold in Honduras, lived in poverty in Buenos Aires and in New York's Greenwich Village, and acted in his father's company. While working in Connecticut as a newspaper reporter, he contracted tuberculosis. During his lengthy recovery he reviewed his life and decided to write for the theater. "I want to be an artist," he wrote, "or nothing."

O'Neill first won recognition with short plays, like *Ile*, which dealt with life at sea. They were moody plays with tragic overtones, very different from the romantic and sentimental dramas performed by his father. "The theater to me *is* life," O'Neill argued, "and life is struggle."

Beyond the Horizon, his first important full-length drama, was produced on Broadway in 1920 and was awarded the Pulitzer Prize for that year. From this point in his career until his death in 1953, O'Neill experimented with themes and techniques: flashbacks in *The Emperor Jones*, masks in *The Great God Brown*, stream-of-consciousness in *Strange Interlude*, and Greek myth in *Mourning Becomes Electra*. His themes focused on man's search for spiritual truths, and he became known for creating characters of great psychological depth and complexity. The novelist Sinclair Lewis wrote that O'Neill had almost single-handedly changed the American theater "from a false world of neat and competent trickery, to a world of splendor, and fear, and greatness."

The climax of O'Neill's career came in 1936 when he was awarded the Nobel Prize in Literature. He was the second American (Lewis was first) and the only American dramatist to be so honored. The later plays, such as *The Iceman Cometh* (1948) and *Long Day's Journey into Night* (not performed until 1956, three years after his death) brought his work to a new generation of playgoers. *Long Day's Journey*, which was made into a motion picture, is the most autobiographical of O'Neill's plays. It deals with a family of four — a father who is an actor, a mother who is a morphine addict, and two sons who are tortured by the air of tragedy and doom that engulfs the family.

O'Neill is now recognized as one of the outstanding innovators in twentieth-century drama. He was the most powerful of the many American playwrights (including Thornton Wilder, Maxwell Anderson, William Saroyan, and Tennessee Williams) who have gone beyond the superficial conventions of realistic drama. His goal was a personal one, he once explained: "Is it the truth as I know it, or better still feel it? If so, shoot, and let the splinters fly where they will."

Study Guide

1. What is "ile"? What special meaning does it have for Keeney?
2. What is Keeney's reputation on board the *Atlantic Queen?* in home port?
3. In what ways does each of the following adjectives apply to Captain Keeney's character — (a) proud, (b) selfish, (c) loving, (d) obsessed?
4. Why did Annie accompany her husband on this voyage? What does she discover? What effect do these discoveries have on her?
5. What indications do you find that Keeney is sincere when he promises his wife to return to home port? How do you account for his abrupt change of heart?
6. Captain Keeney's final decision is to continue his search for ile. How will the extended voyage affect Annie? the crew? Keeney himself? How does O'Neill suggest their fate at the end?

7. Tragedy often involves a heroic man. He may not be perfect, completely noble, honorable, and wise, but he is engaged in a heroic struggle. Against insuperable odds, he fights to achieve his dream. Did you find Captain Keeney at all heroic? Explain.

Interaction

1. At the climax of *Ile* Captain Keeney is faced with a difficult moral choice: whether to place his wife's needs — and his marriage — above his own needs — his career. Debate the following statements about the Captain's choice:
   a) Keeney is not truly in love with his wife, nor is he deeply moved with her suffering. His decision to be "a good husband" and "to prove a man" are only excuses for indulging his own stubbornness, ambition, and pride.
   b) Keeney desperately needs to get a full cargo of oil, at whatever cost to himself and to others, to meet his own sense of dignity and responsibility as a man and as a husband. He had no honorable choice but to act as he did.

2. Shortly after *Ile* first opened, one reviewer wrote in praise of O'Neill:

   He knows life. . . . He knows the people of the sea and their women. He has a feeling for irony, for the sardonic humor with which the gods plot the drama of human affairs. He knows not only how his people talk, but what they feel and what they hope and how destiny mocks their pathetic ambitions.

   Do you agree with this review? Do you find examples in the play where the hopes and feelings of Captain Keeney and his wife are "mocked" by "destiny"?

Musée des Beaux Arts

Text page 330

W. H. AUDEN   *born:* 1907

Wystan Hugh Auden was educated at Oxford University in England, where he became associated with a group of young poets who rebelled against the upper class establishment. In 1937 Auden went to Spain to work for the Loyalists during the Spanish Civil War. Two years later he came to the United States as a permanent resident and later became a citizen. "The attractiveness of America to a writer," he wrote, "is its openness and lack of tradition. . . . There is no past. No tradition. No roots — that is, in the European sense. . . . But what is happening here is happening everywhere."

In addition to his many volumes of poetry and prose, Auden has written about music and painting and has made many translations. His poetry is noted for its pungent satire; it is poetry with a social conscience. Some of his poems are "September 1, 1939," "On the Death of W. B. Yeats," "Elegy for J. F. K.," and "The Unknown Citizen." (The last appears on text page 655.)

Breughel's painting (line 14) was based on the Greek myth of Daedalus and Icarus, the father and son who tried to escape from the island of Crete on wings made of feathers and wax. According to the myth, as Icarus flew too close to the sun the wings melted and he fell into the sea and drowned. Breughel's painting shows Icarus falling into the sea. But he is very tiny and easy to miss at first glance. The surrounding landscape and objects are larger and easier to see. A plowman and a shepherd in the foreground go about their usual tasks, and a ship continues on its course, as Icarus falls to his death.

Study Guide

1. Lines 5 through 8 pose a contrast between young and old, a contrast that was suggested to the poet as he looked at the paintings in the museum. What is "the miraculous birth" for which the old "passionately" wait? The *it* in line 7 also refers to "the miraculous birth" but in a somewhat different sense. What contrast between young and old does Auden draw in these lines?
2. The speaker says that the "Old Masters" were right about human suffering. What does Breughel's painting say to him about human suffering?
3. Is this poem a protest against anything, or does it accept human nature for what it is? Debate and discuss your answer.

Interaction

As we go about our daily business, most of us ignore or are unaware of the suffering of others. What are some arguments for and against our deep involvement with all human suffering?

Acquainted with the Night

Text page 331

<small>ROBERT FROST</small> 1875–1963

Although he is often thought of as a poet who celebrates nature, Robert Frost has penetrated beneath the beautiful New England countryside to the indifference and stubbornness of nature. Frost, like the nineteenth-century New England poets (pages 352–355), probes the relationship between man and nature, and a moment of decision or insight in Frost's poetry usually occurs in the woods. But Frost has a Yankee earthiness rather than a mystical exaltation in the presence of nature. Like Hawthorne and Emily Dickinson (see pages 723–726), Frost presents mystery instead of ecstasy, irony instead of lofty morals.

Robert Frost was born in San Francisco and later settled in New England, the region with which he is now identified. He tried many occupations, including farming and schoolteaching, and worked in the mills of Lawrence, Massachusetts, until he sold his first poem, "My Butterfly." A married man with a child, a failure as a farmer, and a poet with few prospects, Frost decided to sell his farm and go to England. There he established a reputation as a poet, and back home in America people began to read his collections. There, too, he met Ezra Pound, who encouraged and influenced more writers than any other twentieth-century figure, but Frost was too independent to continue long under the wing of the "maestro."

Frost and his family returned to America just before the outbreak of World War I. The publication of *A Boy's Will* brought him from obscurity to best-seller status. Frost was forty-one, but his powers had not yet reached their peak. He lived in rural New England, lectured at Amherst, and continued for more than four decades to be one of the few poets actually read by average Americans. He was quoted as no writer since Longfellow had been: "Two roads diverged in a wood, and I — /I took the one less traveled by,/And that has made all the difference"; "And miles to go before I sleep"; "Some say the world will end in fire,/Some say in ice" were some lines that won Frost the unofficial title of Poet Laureate of the United States. By 1961 he had become such a national institution that he was asked to read a poem at the inauguration of President John F. Kennedy.

Although popular with readers, Frost at first met with mixed reaction from critics. To some, Frost was an old-fashioned poet and a regional poet. While it was fashionable to experiment with verse form and typography, Frost used conventional rhyme and meter. His poems so exuded the atmosphere of New England that some critics missed their universality. But Frost's verse eventually came to be recognized as some of the greatest poetry of this century. Randall Jarrell, a younger poet and an admirer of Frost, has summed up Frost's independence of spirit and universality:

Frost is that rare thing, a complete or representative poet, and not one of the brilliant partial poets who do justice, far more than justice, to a portion of reality, and leave the rest of things forlorn. When you know Frost's poems you know surprisingly well how the world seemed to one man, and what it was to seem that way. . . . The grimness and awfulness and untouchable sadness of things, both in the world and in the self, have justice done to them in the poems, but no more justice than is done to the tenderness and love and delight. . . .

Comment

I think of Robert Frost as a terrifying poet. Call him, if it makes things any easier, a tragic poet, but it might be useful every now and then to come out from under the shelter of that literary word. The universe that he conceives is a terrifying universe.

— LIONEL TRILLING: A Speech on Robert Frost

Study Guide

1. Robert Frost is usually associated with the rural, sparsely inhabited countryside of New England. Where does this poem seem to take place?
2. As the speaker passes the night watchman, what is it that he is unwilling to explain?
3. Notice that the first and last lines of the poem are identical. But before we reach the last line, we read about the "interrupted cry," which seems meaningless to the speaker; and we read about the clock, which is no more helpful in guiding him than anything else he meets with. What additional meaning does the phrase "acquainted with the night" convey to you when it is repeated?
4. What kinds of human experience does "night" represent to the speaker?

5. The speaker does not tell us what has happened to him, nor what specific events have made him "acquainted with the night." Does this mystery make the poem less powerful, or more powerful? Why?

Dark Voices in American Literature: Summing Up

1. In his *Notebooks* Hawthorne defined the Unpardonable Sin as he saw it. Which of man's basic wrongs or weaknesses do the following authors probe?
   a) Thomas Hooker and Jonathan Edwards
   b) Edgar Allan Poe
   c) William Melvin Kelley
   d) Oliver La Farge
   e) Walter Van Tilburg Clark
   f) Eugene O'Neill
   g) W. H. Auden
2. The British author D. H. Lawrence advised readers to look through the surface of American art and see the "inner diabolism of the symbolic meaning." "Otherwise," he said, "it is all childishness." How do the following symbols represent what Lawrence called "inner diabolism"?
   a) the forest and the clouds ("Young Goodman Brown")
   b) the house ("The Fall of the House of Usher")
   c) the silence and the ice floes (*Ile*)
   d) the night ("Acquainted with the Night")
   e) the lead pipe ("The Portable Phonograph")
Do you agree with Lawrence that it is the "inner diabolism" — the dark vision of human nature — that makes these works important, that without this "inner diabolism" they would simply be childish?

VOICES OF AFFIRMATION

Remarks upon Receiving the Nobel Prize

Text pages 335–336

WILLIAM FAULKNER   (biography pages 125–126)

Comment

. . . Faulkner himself took the initiative in the criticism of his own work. He was asked to explain to himself and to his admirers the meaning of what he had been saying in the past twenty-five years. . . . The wonder grew that this man who had described so powerfully and so frequently the ugly, chaotic, miserable, obscene, irrational world of man should have meant all along that he was upholding the "old virtues". . . .

—HOFFMAN *and* VICKERY: William Faulkner:
Three Decades of Criticism

Study Guide

1. What does Faulkner mean by the "old verities and . . . universal truths"? Why have they been forgotten?
2. What does Faulkner believe makes man immortal?
3. What does Faulkner believe is the writer's duty?

Interaction

1. As the **Comment** above shows, many Americans were surprised at Faulkner's Stockholm speech. His stories and novels seem concerned with violence, decay, and horror rather than compassion, endurance, and hope. But reevaluation revealed these affirmative themes in Faulkner's writing. In what ways, if any, are the following "dark voices" also voices of affirmation?
    a) Nathaniel Hawthorne (page 187)
    b) Thomas Hooker (page 267)
    c) Walter Van Tilburg Clark (page 307)
    d) W. H. Auden (page 330)

2. Who are some writers you have read who you feel create "out of the materials of the human spirit something which did not exist before"? Name some writers who in your opinion write about "the problems of the human heart in conflict with itself."

from The Autobiography of Benjamin Franklin

Letter to Joseph Priestley

Text pages 337–340

BENJAMIN FRANKLIN   1706–1790

A list of the works of Benjamin Franklin tells a great deal about the man. A diplomat, economist, and scientist, he was one of the authors of the Articles of Confederation, set down a basic theory of capitalism, and contributed to modern electronics. But no practical problem was too small for this man of reason and wit, for he also wrote *Observations on the Causes and Cures of Smoky Chimneys, The Art of Swimming,* and *The Morals of Chess.*

Born only three years after Jonathan Edwards, Franklin began his remarkable career as a printer's apprentice. Before long he had his own print shop and was publisher of the *Pennsylvania Gazette. Poor Richard's Almanack* first appeared in 1732 and immediately became popular for its mixture of practical advice and witty sayings. At one time or another, Franklin was engaged in trade, selling soap, cheese, rags, lottery tickets, and a cure for the itch. Soon Franklin was rich enough to retire, and he often urged men of ambition to follow his example of thrift, hard work, and shrewdness if they too wished to grow rich. It is this Franklin that writer D. H. Lawrence and others attack for being too materialistic.

But Franklin had only begun to find outlets for his energy and brilliance. He initiated civic improvements, such as a circulating library for Philadelphia, and conducted his now legendary experiment with the kite and the key. In 1757 he entered international politics as the Pennsylvania Assembly's representative in England. There he observed English conduct in world affairs and wrote a satire, "Rules by Which a Great Empire May Be Reduced to a Small One." When he returned to America in 1775, he joined Jefferson and

John Adams in drafting the Declaration of Independence. He was then dispatched to France to win support for the Revolution and was a huge popular success as well as a shrewd negotiator. He performed his final public service as a delegate to the Constitutional Convention.

The image of Ben Franklin has been somewhat deadened by his stature as a "founding father" after whom an untold number of schools in the United States have been named. But Franklin was very much a human being and was never so much aware of it as when he set out to write his *Autobiography*. In this book he talks about his weaknesses, his vanity, his vices. He preaches virtue and moderation in all things and reports, rather naively at times, his struggles to overcome his pride; "even if I could conceive that I had completely overcome it," he wrote, "I should probably be proud of my humility."

Study Guide

1. Judging from these short passages from his *Autobiography*, what can you say about Franklin's personality and interests?
2. In the first selection from his *Autobiography* Franklin suggests that "there is some inconsistency in our common mode of teaching languages." (page 338) What seems inconsistent to him? What improvement does he suggest? What "circumstances" led him to this suggestion?
3. What problems is Franklin concerned with in "A Plan for Philadelphia"? What solution does he offer? What was the final solution to this problem? What does this plan reveal about Franklin?

Interaction

1. One critic of Benjamin Franklin has called his career "a colossal misfortune to the United States," because our country seems to have adopted Franklin's belief in material progress as *the* American way of life. Where in the *Autobiography* and in the letter to Priestley is Franklin concerned with material progress? Do you feel that Franklin's faith in material progress has been justified?
2. Do we still share Franklin's unbounded faith in progress through science? What has happened since Franklin's time which might give us a different view of technical achievements? Have we made any progress in "moral science"? Have men in any way ceased "to be wolves to one another"?

Education for Democracy

Text pages 341–342

THOMAS JEFFERSON   1743–1826

Like Franklin, Thomas Jefferson was uniquely aware of the challenge of his times, and like Franklin, too, he was amazingly versatile: he was a lawyer, a scientist, an architect, an inventor, a politician, a writer, a diplomat, and a President of the United States. His greatest accomplishments in his own estimation were the Declaration of Independence, the Virginia Statute for Religious Freedom, and the founding of the University of Virginia.

Jefferson was born to an aristocratic Southern family. After college he lived the life of a country gentleman, managing his estate and engaging in local politics. When he was chosen to draft the Declaration of Independence, he borrowed from many philosophers who advocated personal freedom and believed in the "contract" between the government and the governed. Jefferson's own idealism and "eternal hostility against every form of tyranny over the mind of man" gave form to one of the most important documents in the nation's history.

Shortly before Franklin began the second installment of his *Autobiography* in 1784, Jefferson composed his *Notes on the State of Virginia*. Besides being a champion of political independence, Jefferson sought to free American society from the aristocratic traditions of England.

Comment

He was a master of English style, and his words ring with conviction and sincerity even though they lack the whimsy and variety of the more devious Franklin.

The essence of Jefferson's thought lies in his faith in the integrity of the individual man. On this foundation he built his structure of government and society with a minimum of arbitrary controls. His purpose was to make the experiment of free government so successful that it would be an example to the rest of the world and a moral force in the destiny of mankind. The principles of decentralization of authority, agrarian economy, public education, and flexible laws were all by-products of the central doctrine of perfectibility.

— ROBERT E. SPILLER: The Cycle of American Literature

Study Guide

1. In what ways does Jefferson try to suit the school system to the age, the capacity, and the economic condition of all the people? Why does Jefferson stress the teaching of history?
2. What are the ultimate goals of Jefferson's proposals?

Interaction

1. In your own words, why is universal education necessary if a democracy is to function?
2. Do you believe that most Americans have enough information to cast their votes intelligently? Why or why not?
3. To what extent has Jefferson's ideal of democracy come into being? To what extent does it still remain to be achieved?

Self-Reliance

Text pages 343–348

RALPH WALDO EMERSON   1803–1882

There was nothing unusual about the audience at the Harvard Phi Beta Kappa Society meeting on August 31, 1837. Nor did the shy speaker with the birdlike face suggest that either he or his subject — "The American Scholar" — would prevent the audience from catching forty winks. But when the talk was over, the listeners were aware that a revolution had begun, and that Ralph Waldo Emerson was its standard-bearer.

Emerson's rebellion against traditional thought was the result of a long and sometimes painful process. He came from a poor family; many of them were doomed to death by tuberculosis. He fell in love with the delicate Ellen Tucker, who died one year after their marriage. He sought comfort in books and introspection, and finally put himself through Harvard's divinity school. His modest success as a clergyman seemed assured. Then suddenly he resigned from the ministry.

His resignation was a protest, first, against the church's authority over the individual's spiritual life and, second, against the growing materialism in America. He began to spread his new ideas, inspiring young men like Thoreau (see text page 597) and captivating a culture-hungry America with the force of his personal conviction.

Emerson's belief in intellectual freedom kept him from constructing a logical or practical system. Instead, he created an atmosphere of experiment, in which rebellion against religious, literary, and governmental authority were embraced as healthy expressions of the individual and divine spirit. His message — conveyed in lyrical, vague, and sometimes mystical prose — was optimistic: man was to have faith in himself, in other men, and in the universe.

Emerson's message had developed out of his youthful poverty, his loss of a wife and two younger brothers, his talks with English writers, his readings in romantic poetry and Eastern philosophy, and a host of other experiences. By 1840 he was lecturing and writing widely on his philosophy, which had become known as Transcendentalism. As he presents it, Transcendentalism is a mixture of the romantic and the practical, the spiritual and the natural. To fulfill his human and divine destiny, according to Emerson, a man must throw off the shackles of authority and the taboos of society; at the same time, a man must earn a living (Emerson's ancestors included hard-headed businessmen as well as scholars and ministers). Man must go beyond the senses — rely on intuition — to achieve a oneness with the divine spirit; using the senses in the study of nature would lead man to this ultimate spiritual unity. Contradictory? Perhaps, but Emerson believed that "A foolish consistency is the hobgoblin of little minds. . . . With consistency a great soul has simply nothing to do."

Comments

If any other man should adopt this method of composition, the result would be incomprehensible chaos; because most men have many interests, many moods, many and conflicting ideas. But with Emerson it was otherwise. There was only one thought which could set him aflame, and that was the thought of the unfathomed might of man. This thought was his religion, his politics, his ethics, his philosophy. One moment of inspiration was in him brother to the next moment of inspiration, although they might be separated by six weeks. When he came to put together his star-born ideas, they fitted well, no matter in what order he placed them, because they were all part of the same idea.

— JOHN JAY CHAPMAN: Emerson

. . . Emerson's idealism was double-edged: it was concerned not merely with the spiritual life of the individual, but also with the individual in society, with the "conduct of life." This latter aspect of his teaching was in fact the secret of his contemporary influence. For if the logical result of a thoroughgoing, self-reliant individualism in the world of the spirit is to become a saint, it is no less true that the logical result of a thoroughgoing, self-reliant individualism in the world of the flesh is to become a millionaire. And in fact it would be hard to say whether Emerson more keenly relished saintliness or shrewdness. Both qualities he himself possessed in a high degree, as only an American can; and if on one side of his nature he was a most lonely and beautiful seer, the records of his life prove that he lacked none of the sagacity and caution of the true Yankee husbandman. He perfectly combined the temperaments of Jonathan Edwards and Benjamin Franklin; — the upper and lower levels of the American mind are fused in him and each becomes the sanction of the other.

— VAN WYCK BROOKS: Our Poets

Study Guide

1. In Emerson's view, how do each of the following tend to undermine self-reliance?
   a) imitating others
   b) society
   c) philanthropy
   d) consistency
   e) property
2. Emerson attacks the idea that the individual is ultimately responsible to his society. In your opinion is the term "self-reliance," as Emerson uses it, a synonym for selfishness? Explain.
3. What faith does Emerson affirm in the following statements?
   a) "We but half express ourselves, and are ashamed of that divine idea which each of us represents." (page 343)
   b) "Accept the place the divine providence has found for you. . . ." (page 343)
   c) "We lie in the lap of immense intelligence, which makes us receivers of its truth and organs of its activity." (page 346)
   d) "That which each can do best, none but his Maker can teach him." (page 347)
4. In Emerson's view, to whom is a man ultimately responsible? How does insisting "on yourself" carry out "that divine idea which each of us represents"?

Interaction

1. Debate the following provocative assertions in "Self-Reliance":
   a) "Whoso would be a man, must be a nonconformist." (page 344)
   b) "Good and bad are but names . . . the only right is what is after my constitution; the only wrong is what is against it." (page 344)
   c) ". . . your miscellaneous popular charities; the education at college of fools; . . . alms to sots, and the thousand-fold Relief Societies — though I confess with shame I sometimes succumb and give the dollar, it is a wicked dollar. . . ." (pages 344–345)
   d) "To be great is to be misunderstood." (page 346)
2. What do you think Emerson might have said if he had read Franklin's "Letter to Joseph Priestley"? With what ideas would he have been most likely to agree? To what ideas would he probably have taken exception?

---

from Nature

Text pages 349–351

RALPH WALDO EMERSON (biography pages 93–94)

Study Guide

1. Emerson warns that "Empirical science is apt to cloud the sight. . . ." (page 349) What does *empirical* mean? How, according to Emerson, can science mislead?
2. How does Emerson feel the "true naturalist" looks at nature?

Interaction

What are Emerson's attitudes toward the following?
   a) reason and intuition
   b) natural facts and spiritual facts
   c) science and religion

Three New England Poets: Bryant, Holmes, and Longfellow

Comment

I call them the schoolroom poets because they were a literary staple of the curriculum in schools until the last two decades and because they are still a familiar serving. Their faces in steel engravings have long gazed benignly — though to many students with torpidness and enmity even — from the schoolroom walls. And not merely the schoolroom belonged to them but often the whole building. At some time or other most Americans have attended a school named Bryant, Whittier, Holmes, Lowell, or Longfellow.

No matter what we think of these poets they are probably more widely known from early learning and general currency than any other group of authors in America. That is the great literary fact about them — their pervasiveness. . . . Whether a good thing or bad, that may not be so in another twenty years. Our nineteenth-century poets are being almost completely ignored by present-day criticism. As for the schoolroom, if they are not being displaced by Frost, Stevens, W. C. Williams, Eliot, and Ransom, they are yielding to picture books and television.

— George Arms: The Fields Were Green

To a Waterfowl

Text page 353

William Cullen Bryant   1794–1878

William Cullen Bryant was the product of a puritanical Massachusetts family. He developed early the habit of exploring the splendid forests of the Berkshire Mountains. As a teenager he wrote nature poems and felt the closeness with nature that the English romantic poet William Wordsworth had expressed. At seventeen Bryant composed one of his most famous nature poems, "Thanatopsis," in which he asks, "How shall I face death?" Years later, when the poem was submitted to the *North American Review*, the editor assumed it had been written by an English poet. "No one on this side of the Atlantic," he said, "is capable of writing such verse."

Bryant's family, finding Harvard and Yale too liberal in religion, sent him to a nearby college to study law. There the rebellious young Bryant read romantic poetry and frequented taverns.

One afternoon in December 1815, Bryant set out across a field. He was twenty-one and about to open a law office in Plainfield, Massachusetts. This walk was to prove a crucial moment in Bryant's life, for as he walked, alone and uncertain of his future, he saw a waterfowl silhouetted against the evening sky. Deeply moved, Bryant saw the bird's flight as nature's affirmation of divine goodness and power. Later he composed a poetic record of this moment — "To a Waterfowl."

Bryant grew dissatisfied with practicing law, which he called the "drudge for the dregs of men," and went to New York. There he became editor and part owner of the *Evening Post*. He wrote little poetry at this time, directing most of his energies toward the crusade against slavery. His editorials on many subjects, often highly moral in tone, were courageous and honest, and made him one of the great figures in American journalism.

Study Guide

1. What danger does Bryant think of in stanza 2?
2. Bryant affirms that "There is a Power" that guides the bird in its flight. He mentions this again at the end of the poem in the lines "He who, from zone to zone,/. . . Will lead my steps aright." What "Power" is Bryant referring to in these lines?
3. In stanza 7 Bryant says that the waterfowl has taught him a lesson. The lesson is explained in stanza 8. Explain the lesson in your own words.
4. In stanza 8 it becomes clear that Bryant is comparing himself with the waterfowl. Reread the poem, keeping this comparison in mind. What is Bryant's mood as he writes stanzas 1 through 5? What questions has he probably been asking himself?
5. **Style.** Each stanza in the poem is a single, complicated sentence. What is the plain sense of the first stanza? Restate Bryant's question in your own words. Bryant also uses uncommon words, words that are not often used in speech. What unusual words or combinations of words do you find in the poem? What is your reaction to Bryant's style?

The Chambered Nautilus

Text page 354

OLIVER WENDELL HOLMES 1809–1894

Oliver Wendell Holmes studied medicine in Europe, then returned to practice and teach it in Cambridge, Massachusetts. Holmes was a Unitarian, in revolt against the Calvinist doctrine of inherited guilt. "If for the Fall of man," he wrote, "science comes to substitute the Rise of man, sir, it means the utter disintegration of all the spiritual pessimisms which have been like a spasm in the heart and a cramp in the intellect of man for so many centuries."

A merry and light-hearted man, Holmes frequently enlivened his medical lectures with puns and witty stories. His charm and poetic bent encouraged his classmates and students at Harvard to call on him to write occasional verse. Because it was written for class reunions and banquets, his occasional verse is not widely read today. But he was a versatile writer, turning out prose essays for the *Atlantic Monthly,* meditative verse like "Contentment," and humorous poetry like "The Height of the Ridiculous." His protest poem, "Old Ironsides," which first brought him fame, was written when he was a graduate student; the poem protested the destruction of the *Constitution,* a War of 1812 frigate, and the ship was saved.

"The Chambered Nautilus," which shows Holmes's combined interest in science and poetry, was originally included in *The Autocrat of the Breakfast-Table.* In this series of essays, Dr. Holmes is thinly disguised as the "autocrat," who leads lively discussions with a group of boardinghouse residents. The success of *Autocrat* led to *The Professor at the Breakfast-Table* and *The Poet at the Breakfast-Table.* These works reflect the vitality one of Holmes's friends recognized when he said, "Holmes, you are intellectually the most alive man I ever knew." Holmes replied, "I am, I am! From the crown of my head to the sole of my foot, I'm alive, I'm alive!"

Like Bryant, who learns a lesson from the waterfowl, Holmes learns a lesson from the sea shell. During its lifetime the sea mollusk builds a shell around itself, then leaves this chamber to build another and larger one on top of the old one. Thus, this particular sea shell has several chambers, each one larger than the last.

Study Guide

1. What romantic picture does Holmes paint in stanza 1? Why does Holmes say in stanza 2, "Wrecked is the ship of pearl"?
2. What process does Holmes describe in stanza 3?
3. "Thanks for the heavenly message brought by thee," Holmes writes, speaking to the chambered nautilus. He explains the message in the next stanza. Express this message in your own words.
4. How would you define the "stately mansions" the poet urges his soul to build? Obviously he does not mean "houses" in the ordinary sense.

The Sound of the Sea

Text page 355

Henry Wadsworth Longfellow   1807–1882

Henry Wadsworth Longfellow was the most widely read American poet of his own time. Not only Americans read his ballads by the fireside; in Europe he was quoted everywhere, and England honored him by placing a memorial to him in Westminster Abbey, not far from the memorials to Milton, Chaucer, and Shakespeare.

Longfellow attended Bowdoin College in Maine. After travel and study in Europe he returned to America as a teacher, first at Bowdoin, later at Harvard. Translating European works contributed to the development of his characteristic style — simple and musical. But it wasn't long before Longfellow began to adapt European forms to American materials. In 1839 he wrote "The Wreck of the Hesperus," a ballad in the centuries-old tradition of Europe. *"The national ballad,"* Longfellow wrote, "is a virgin soil like New England; and there are great materials." Many other famous ballads followed, among them "The Courtship of Miles Standish," based on the romance of Longfellow's ancestor John Alden; "The Song of Hiawatha," "Paul Revere's Ride," and "The Village Blacksmith." These ballads are still read, and most Americans can still quote:

> Why don't you speak for yourself, John?
>
> I shot an arrow into the air,
> It fell to earth, I know not where.

Under the spreading chestnut tree,
The village smithy stands.

This is the forest primeval.

Listen, my children, and you shall hear
Of the midnight ride of Paul Revere.

"The Sound of the Sea" is a meditative lyric rather than a ballad. It is a sonnet in the mood for which the "Cambridge group" and the "Concord group" became famous. The contemplation of nature leads the poet to an insight into his own and the divine spirit.

Study Guide

1. Longfellow begins by describing "the rising tide." How does he describe "the sound of the sea"? How does he convey a sense of mystery?
2. To what does Longfellow compare "the rising tide" in the final six lines of the poem?

Interaction

1. The poems of Bryant, Holmes, and Longfellow are in the didactic tradition. That is, each poem carries a clear spiritual message. Do you object to having the poet explain his message to you? Why or why not? Suppose the final stanzas were omitted from "To a Waterfowl" and "The Chambered Nautilus." What do you think would be lost? What would be gained? Does the message of each poem strike you as "preachy"? Why or why not?
2. In what ways do Bryant, Holmes, and Longfellow share Emerson's attitude toward nature?

Walt Whitman 1819–1892

(biography text pages 356–357)

Comments

A great poet once loved America with such passion that the whole of it was constantly before his eyes. And what he could not see of it he heard; and what he could not hear of it he touched. Walt Whitman's delight in his country was so enormous and so simple that he could not bear the thought of its absence from him. This is why his poems are so full of the names of things: of rivers, of states, of cities and tools and occupations. He is always itemizing his love, calling it by its myriad titles, bringing it home to his senses so that it shall not escape him and grow cool. No man ever loved his land at closer range, or ever said so more eloquently.

All of it was about him all the time. He possessed in supreme degree the power of pausing and listening to the great life beyond oneself. At this moment, now, his poems seem to say, while I, Walt Whitman, sit in my Brooklyn boardinghouse or stand at the prow of a ferry which is puffing toward Manhattan, a woodsman in Michigan is lifting his ax; an engineer along the Mohawk is peering at his gauges; a slave in the rice fields is bending over his sack; clerks are hurrying to their offices in St. Louis; an officer is barking commands at his soldiers on the Indian frontier; Indians are slipping their fishing canoes into the northwestern waters; a man is bringing meat home in brown paper; a baby is going to sleep in its mother's arms; lovers are strolling; an old woman is dying in an Allegheny cabin; factories are smoking, whistles are getting ready to blow, the rivers are rushing through their valleys, the fish are quiet in their pools, an eagle is measuring the Rocky Mountains with its wing, and the philosopher is frowning at his desk. Walt Whitman himself was by trade a newspaperman in Brooklyn and New York, nor was he particularly successful at his trade. But his calling was wider. It was the breathing and beautiful earth, whose manifold realities he slowly fashioned into an original kind of poetry to celebrate. *Leaves of Grass* in its various editions, from the first in 1855 to the last which he saw through the press in 1891–1892, is the testament of his love; and it is a book through which Americans have continued to feel, hear, see, touch, and smell their country, and to find it good.
— MARK VAN DOREN

The beastliness of the author is set forth in his own description of himself, and we can conceive of no better reward than the lash for such a violation of decency. . . . He must be some escaped lunatic raving in pitiable delirium.
— *The Boston Intelligencer*, 1855

He is, in "Song of Myself," the only really "free" American. He is, or seems to be, beyond good and evil, beyond the compulsion to pit his ideals against history and social reality. Cooper, Melville, Mark Twain are never so transcendently free; their dreams are troubled and their having dreams makes them sad and guilty; they impose upon us the weary task of moral judgment and upon themselves a willed and rhetorical self-justification. And if Whitman affords a welcome contrast to our American moralists, he also floods the ego with a vital gaiety of a special quality unknown to Europe.

— RICHARD CHASE, 1955

Study Guide

from "Song of Myself," *text pages* 358–364

1. **Part 1.** What picture of himself does Whitman give in these lines? How is he representative? How does he intend to represent nature? (See the final stanza.)

2. **Part 6.** The question "What is the grass?" is not answered with a scientific or a dictionary definition. What answers does Whitman suggest?

3. **Part 9.** What is the scene of this section? the mood? Which words and phrases appeal to the senses? How does he develop his earlier statement, "I harbor . . ./Nature without check with original energy"?

4. **Part 12.** In part 6 Whitman spoke of "a uniform hieroglyphic." In what ways does part 12 explain the "uniform hieroglyphic"? How does this section express a "democratic vision"?

5. **Part 17.** "This is the grass . . ./This is the common air" are metaphors. To what does *this* refer in each statement? What does Whitman imply is the purpose of his poems?

6. **Part 24.** In this section Whitman portrays himself as a mythic poet; that is, he claims that the universal is expressing itself through his person, his voice. Is this egotism, or is it the reverse of egotism? Explain.

7. **Part 33.** In this section Whitman writes, "I understand the large hearts of heroes, . . ./The disdain and calmness of martyrs." What examples does he give of "heroes" and "martyrs"? What is Whitman's feeling toward humanity?

8. **Part 48.** How do you interpret the line, "And whoever walks a furlong without sympathy walks to his own funeral drest in his shroud"? Whitman writes, "I hear and behold God in every object, yet understand God not in the least." Does Whitman think it is necessary or important to *understand* God? Why or why not?

9. **Part 51.** How does Whitman address the reader and talk to him personally? What does he invite the reader to do? What is Whitman's attitude toward his reader?
10. **Part 52.** In *Leaves of Grass* Whitman calls himself "an American, one of the roughs. . . ." How does Whitman portray himself as "one of the roughs" in this part? Which lines show his enthusiasm for the natural and primitive? Whitman writes, "I depart as air. . . . I bequeath myself to the dirt. . . ." Where else in "Song of Myself" does Whitman identify himself with common aspects of nature?

"Sparkles from the Wheel," *text pages 364–365*

The next two poems are similar to each other in structure. (They also recall the poems of the New England poets.) The first part of each poem concerns something that Whitman saw. The second part of each describes what he felt about what he saw.

1. What scene does Whitman describe in the first part of the poem?
2. In the second part of the poem, Whitman becomes very involved in watching the knife grinder at work. He describes himself as "a phantom curiously floating, now here absorb'd and arrested." How is Whitman reacting to the scene?
3. The sparkles are the focal point of the scene; they are juxtaposed with the individuals who form a crowd around the knife grinder. The poet suggests a comparison here. How is the life of each man like a sparkle from the wheel?

"As Toilsome I Wander'd Virginia's Woods," *text page 365*

1. What did Whitman find as he walked through the forest?
2. When does he recall this scene?
3. How does the discovery of the rough inscription first affect the speaker? When Whitman repeats the inscription ("Bold, cautious, true, and my loving comrade"), he indicates that it now has a special significance. What do you think is its special significance?
4. Whitman spent some time during the Civil War searching for his brother, a soldier in the Union Army. He also visited the wounded (both Union and Confederate), comforting them with

food, books, and, as one writer says, "the 'magnetism' of his personality." How do these facts help explain why Whitman cannot forget the scene in Virginia's woods?

"I Hear America Singing," *text page 366*
1. Whitman mentions the carpenter, the mason, the woodcutter and others; he does not mention here (as he does in other poems) the banker, the politician, or the professor. Why does Whitman select the former only? Why do these people, and not the banker, the politician, and the professor, represent America to Whitman? Do you think Whitman's America is idealized? Explain.
2. Why does he describe America as *singing?*
3. Whitman has been both praised and criticized for his "lists." What is the effect of listing the people and their songs? Where in "Song of Myself" does Whitman use a "list"? What is your reaction to this poetic technique?

"A Noiseless Patient Spider," *text page 366*
1. Like Bryant and Holmes, Whitman here compares himself, or his soul, to something in nature. In what ways does he resemble the spider?
2. What do the spider's filaments represent? How do they recall the chambered nautilus?
3. What mystical or spiritual experience is Whitman describing here?

Interaction
1. In a stanza not included here, Whitman writes, "I know perfectly well my own egotism." Some of his readers and critics have remarked on Whitman's "egotism." What words and ideas in "Song of Myself" give an impression of "egotism"? Do you think the poem is egotistical? Why or why not?
2. Critic Northrop Frye writes:

Literature associates, by words, the non-human world of physical nature with the human world, and the units of this association are analogy and identity, which appear in the two commonest figures of speech, the simile and the metaphor.

In what ways do "Sparkles from the Wheel" and "A Noiseless Patient Spider" associate the nonhuman and human worlds?

How are the two poems similar in structure and theme? (Note that each poem contains the phrase "vast surrounding.")

3. Compare "A Noiseless Patient Spider" with "To a Waterfowl" and "The Chambered Nautilus." (pages 353–355) What idea do the three poems share?

4. In "Song of Myself" Whitman identifies himself with all of humanity: "I do not ask the wounded person how he feels, I myself become the wounded person." On this identity Whitman builds his theory of democracy. How is this same idea of democracy — of identification with the masses of people — expressed or implied in "Sparkles from the Wheel," "As Toilsome I Wander'd," and "I Hear America Singing"?

5. Loren Eiseley, the naturalist, once observed a spider spinning a web across the globe of a street light on a snowy autumn evening. He writes:

> Her adventure against the great blind forces of winter, her seizure of this warming globe of light, would come to nothing and was hopeless. Nevertheless it brought . . . into my mind . . . a kind of heroism, a world where even a spider refuses to lie down and die if a rope can still be spun on to a star.

Compare this incident with the situation presented in Whitman's "A Noiseless Patient Spider." Compare the attitude of each writer toward "his" spider.

The People Will Live On

Text pages 367–369

CARL SANDBURG   1878–1967 (biography text page 367)

Comment

Sandburg paints a picture of the vital force of a people in many different shades but qualified by the inherent dignity of man in his work, family, friendships, and responsibilities. He also paints with touches of irony other anti-social selfish aspects; he has never lost sympathy. . . .

Sandburg draws upon Emerson for his belief in the sanctity of the individual mind; for the belief that "America is itself a poem"; that the commonplace, the common man are poetic material; that poetry of protest (when protest is called for) is the mark of Man Thinking. He draws also from Thoreau the spirit of protest when non-conformity to custom is not in the interest of the common welfare.

— HAZEL DURNELL: The America of Carl Sandburg

Study Guide

1. How does Sandburg illustrate his assertion that
   a) "the people is a tragic and comic two-face. . . ." (page 368)
   b) "the people is a polychrome. . . ." (page 369)
2. Note that Sandburg says, "The people is," not "The people are." How does this use of *people* as a singular noun explain Sandburg's purpose in the poem?
3. What dimension of human experience does Sandburg describe in lines 26–45?
4. Why, according to Sandburg, will the people live on?

Interaction

1. Compare Sandburg's treatment of the people with Whitman's in "Song of Myself," sections 9, 12, and 33. What differences in "distance" between speaker and subject do you note in the two poems?
2. Both Sandburg and Faulkner in his "Remarks Upon Receiving the Nobel Prize" (page 335) address themselves to the human spirit. Which lines from Sandburg's poem come very close to saying the same thing as Faulkner's "I believe that man will not merely endure: he will prevail"?

Theme for English B

Text pages 370–371

LANGSTON HUGHES   1902–1967

Langston Hughes, one of the most popular of twentieth-century poets, was largely interested in portraying Negro life in America. As a young man he figured prominently in the Harlem Renaissance.

He edited many anthologies which helped make the work of American and African black writers better known. His poems incorporate dialect, humor, and blues rhythms. He also translated poets from Cuba, Haiti, and Mexico, and his own poems have been translated into many languages and set to music. Although he is known best for his poety, Hughes also wrote songs, children's books, short stories, travel articles, movies, and plays.

In many schools a composition or essay written in English class is called a *theme*.

Study Guide

1. Describe the speaker of "Theme for English B."
2. What is he trying to accomplish by writing this "page"?
3. The speaker identifies one part of himself with Harlem. A larger part, he realizes, can be identified with New York City. Who and what else does the speaker accept as a part of his life?
4. The instructor tells him that if his theme is deeply felt and honest it will be "true." Do you think the speaker's "theme" is "true"?
5. In what sense is the voice behind this poem one of affirmation? In what sense not?

Interaction

1. Because the language of this poem is so direct and the situation so particular, the poem may at first appear less universal than it actually is. In fact, it places us face to face with one of the complex issues of American life — that is, the balance between unity and diversity in a large democracy. Undoubtedly the experience of being black in America has been more troubled than that of belonging to other racial and national groups. However, the poem has something to say to all Americans, no matter how we identify our "subculture": as Irish, Italian, Southern, Puerto Rican, Mexican, New England Yankee, to name only a few possibilities. What the poem seems to say is that in order to be American we do not all have to be the same. Yet, paradoxically, in some ways we are all the same, because we spring from American soil and share so much history, whether we like it or not.

On one level the poem is about a student speaking to an instructor. On another level the speaker sees himself as representing all black Americans speaking out to all white Americans. What are the implications, then, of his statement (lines 31–32): "You are white — /yet a part of me, as I am a part of you"?

2. What similarity of theme do you see between this poem and Whitman's "Song of Myself"?

Sale

Text page 371

JOSEPHINE MILES   *born:* 1911

Josephine Miles has taught at the University of California for many years. She divides her interest between poetry and criticism. Her critical prose works are concerned with language analysis. The language of her poetry reflects American speech rhythms in a unique way.

Study Guide

1. Buying a pair of shoes is an unusual subject for a poem, though a commonplace in "real life." What is the mood of the poem? In the last line, is the street itself "perfect," or is it the speaker's mood which makes it seem so?
2. Comment on the language of the poem. Where do you find it to be colloquial? Where do you find the language elevated or formal?
3. Why does the speaker have such admiration for the shoe salesman? Is the poem only about a shoe salesman, or is it about anyone who performs his work or art skillfully?

Voices of Affirmation: Summing Up

1. The writers in this section confront some of the same problems the "dark voices" in the previous section explore, but their ultimate statement is one of faith, hope, affirmation. What specific affirmative beliefs do Franklin, Jefferson, Whitman, and Sandburg express about the promise of America and the progress of all mankind?

2. Unlike the "voices of affirmation," Hawthorne portrays nature as the deep and gloomy forests which conceal witches' ceremonies — as a reflection of evil rather than of divine goodness. What are the main reasons why Emerson, the New England poets, and Whitman look at nature affirmatively? Is their reverence for nature and its benefits to man's knowledge and spirit outdated, or is it pertinent to today? In your answer consider the portrayal of nature in current movies, television shows, and songs.

3. Suppose that you are a reporter interviewing one of the writers in this section. Record the questions you ask and devise answers the author would most likely have given. You may wish to select one of the following topics as the subject of your interview:

    a) The Future of Democracy
    b) The Fight Against Pollution of the Environment
    c) Self-Reliance in the 1970's
    d) Where Science Is Taking Us

STEPHEN CRANE 1871-1900

The brief life of Stephen Crane has become an American legend, that of the young writer who was a celebrity in his own time — adventurous, talented, innocent, and doomed. He helped to create the legend by going on dangerous journalistic missions and making himself a dramatic figure in his dispatches. Like his fictional heroes, Crane lived with hunger and squalor, danger and fear.

Stephen Crane was born in 1871 in Newark, New Jersey, the son of a Methodist minister. School and scholarship never interested him very much, though that was part of the legend too. For instance, he liked to pretend that he was less of a reader than he actually was. In fact, his writing shows that he learned much from the European and American "realists," who tried to present "life as it is," and the "naturalists," who interpreted human behavior in terms of environment.

In his teens, Crane was an outstanding athlete and almost became a professional baseball player. His brother persuaded him to go to college instead. In the spring of 1891, however, he left Syracuse University to get down to the business of becoming a writer.

For a while he worked as a reporter in New Jersey but soon went to New York, where he lived a life of Bohemian poverty. His closest friends in New York were young painters who were strongly influenced by the daring style of the French impressionists. Critics have found that Crane's prose style has much in common with the style of these painters, in whose work bright dabs of color form an "impression" or image of a scene.

Crane's first novel, *Maggie*, was not a success, but *The Red Badge of Courage*, which followed in 1895, made him famous. In spite of his delicate health, he took up the life of a highly paid star reporter. The vigorous life he chose to lead during the next four years almost certainly hastened his early death. In 1896 he set out to see his first war. He reported from Mexico and from the American West. At the same time, he wrote tales based on his travels, one of which is "The Bride Comes to Yellow Sky" (on which James Agee based the movie script, page 68). On a Cuban expedition Crane's ship was wrecked, forcing him and others to drift for days in a small boat. Out of this adventure came the fine story "The Open Boat," and publicity that added to the legend of the courageous young writer. Although the shipwreck had worn his health even more, he traveled to Greece in 1897 to cover the war with Turkey, and then returned to Cuba to cover the Spanish-American War in 1898.

Toward the end of his life, Crane settled down in a manor house in England, where he became friendly with many English writers, including Joseph Conrad. He was living on a grand scale, however, and his debts demanded that he do more and more journalistic writing. His health finally gave way, and in 1900 he died of tuberculosis.

Although Crane wrote at the end of the nineteenth century, his style is close to that of such twentieth-century American writers as Ernest Hemingway. His language is direct and vivid: he wanted to give his readers an immediate sensation of being present at the scene of the action. Hemingway, who shared Crane's fascination with war and adventure, called *The Red Badge of Courage* "that great boy's dream of war that was to be truer to how war is than any war the boy who wrote it would ever live to see. It is one of the finest books of our literature."

Comments

It can be said most confidently that no soldier who fought in our recent War ever saw any approach to the battle scenes in this book — but what wonder? We are told that it is the work of a young man of twenty-three or twenty-four years of age, and so of course must be a mere work of diseased imagination. And yet it constantly strains after so-called realism. The result is a mere riot of words.

— *The Dial,* 1896

Spiritual change, *that* is Henry Fleming's red badge. His red badge is his conscience reborn and purified. Whereas Jim Conklin's red badge of courage is the literal one, the wound of which he dies, Henry's is the psychological badge, the wound of conscience.

— ROBERT WOOSTER STALLMAN

Henry's confident "manhood" at the close depends on externals. His inner voices are hushed. He is a "man" only because his comrades are unaware of his sins. — WINIFRED LYNSKEY

The novel treats four stages in Fleming's growth toward moral maturity. In the beginning he is unable to distinguish between his heroic dreams and hopes and the actual condition of war. Then follows a period of confusion and doubt as reality begins to intrude upon his dream world. Next he goes through a period of desperate but futile struggle to preserve, through deceit and rationalization, his pseudo-heroic image of himself and the world. In the end he solves his problem when he learns to see the world in its true light, when he is finally able to bring his subjectivity into harmony with the reality which his experience makes clear to him.

— JAMES B. COLVERT [1]

The Red Badge of Courage

Text pages 375–491

Study Guide

PRELUDE TO BATTLE — Chapters I–III

1. **Character.** Three characters are the focus of much of the action in the opening chapters. At first, the author does not give these characters names. They remain "the young soldier," "the loud soldier," and "the tall soldier." Even after you discover the names of two of them, the author does not use the names often. What effect does Crane achieve by using adjectives instead of proper names to describe his soldiers? Does he force you to look at them in a certain way?

2. **Character.** How is the youth, Henry, different from the other soldiers? What does Crane tell us about Henry that he does not tell us about the other characters?

3. What were the "new thoughts," the "serious problem" which concerned the youth? How does his conversation with Jim Conklin at the end of Chapter I leave him reassured?

4. In Chapter III Crane writes of Henry: "He was bewildered. . . . He felt carried along by a mob." Throughout the novel Henry is often bewildered, by himself, by the concepts of war and heroism, and by the movements of the army of which he is a tiny

---

[1] From "Structure and Theme in Stephen Crane's Fiction" by J. B. Colvert from *Modern Fiction Studies*, Volume V, Number 3, Autumn 1959, © 1959, by Purdue Research Foundation, Lafayette, Indiana. Reprinted by permission of Purdue Research Foundation.

part. What are some of the points in these opening chapters in which Crane shows the bewilderment of the individual soldier? What causes this bewilderment?

5. What romantic ideas did Henry have about war, glory, and heroism before he actually enlisted? How did the reality of army service upset these ideas? Discuss the following passage from Chapter III: "The youth had been taught that a man became another thing in battle. He saw his salvation in such a change." (page 396) From what does he seek salvation?

6. **Prose style.** The clarity of Crane's prose style has often been admired by other writers, including Ernest Hemingway, whose style Crane influenced. The reader probably does not think of Crane as a "poetic" writer, yet few writers use imagery and color more effectively in prose. Note the opening paragraph describing dawn coming up over the camp. (page 375) Or note the description of the shoes of the dead soldier: "The youth could see that the soles of his shoes had been worn to the thinness of writing paper. . . ." (page 394) Point to some other descriptions in which you find Crane's writing particularly clear or his pictures particularly vivid.

FIRST ENCOUNTER — Chapters IV–VI

1. **Imagery.** At the opening of Chapter V (page 402), Henry is suddenly reminded of a circus parade he watched as a small boy. Why does the circus parade come into his mind? What does this tell us about his attitude toward war, at least in part?

2. How do the realities of this battle compare to the ideas of battle which the youth had had before? During the battle he finds "a singular absence of heroic poses." (page 404) What are some of the unglamorous details of warfare which Crane supplies in his description of battle? Are there any truly "heroic" actions described?

3. **Tone.** What is the tone Crane takes toward Henry's "ecstasy of self-satisfaction"? Does the author appear to agree with Henry "that the man who had fought thus was magnificent"? (page 407) Or is he only reporting the stages of Henry's feelings?

4. **Structure.** The whole novel follows a pattern based on alternating hope and despair. In the opening chapters we have already seen this cycle of hope and despair in Henry's mind. How is that pattern repeated in Chapters V and VI? (See especially pages 407–410.)

5. Why does Henry run during the second attack when he stood his ground the first time? Is he acting as an individual or as a member of a group when he runs?
6. Was Henry's act a cowardly one? Was the running a conscious, voluntary act or was he a victim of some force beyond his control?

DISGRACE — Chapters VII–XIII

1. During these chapters Crane continues the pattern of hope and despair in Henry's mind. The youth must come to terms with himself and with his act of cowardice. Therefore he tries in many ways to justify his act to himself, or to find some turn of events that will vindicate his actions. What are some of the ways in which he tries to justify his behavior? (pages 413–414; 417) Are any of them convincing?
2. **Setting.** In one sense the setting of the novel is the interior of Henry's own mind. In the more obvious sense, it is the landscape in which Henry and his fellow soldiers fight their confused battles. At several points Crane reminds us of one of the great themes of literature: the relation of man to nature. Is nature friendly? unfriendly? or merely neutral? Reread the following passages:
   a) the last paragraph of Chapter V (page 407)
   b) the longer passage at the end of Chapter VII, beginning "He went from the fields into a thick woods. . . ." (pages 414–416
   c) the paragraph beginning "Sometimes the brambles formed chains. . . ." (page 417)
   Discuss the way in which nature (note that Crane capitalizes "nature" in the above paragraphs) plays a role in the novel. How does nature reflect Henry's thoughts and moods? During his retreat to the woods Henry finds a corpse. (page 415) What does the corpse signify to him? What is his reaction?
3. Why does the youth come to regard "the wounded soldiers in an envious way"? (page 421) What pressures or forces led him to the following position:
   "He conceived persons with torn bodies to be peculiarly happy. He wished that he, too, had a wound, a red badge of courage."
4. **Symbol.** Some critics have found religious symbolism in the novel. In particular, they have focused upon the figure of Jim Conklin, even pointing out that his initials may be meant to sug-

gest some parallel to Jesus Christ. Reread the description of Jim Conklin's death (pages 423–425), then tell what details in it might support this concept of Christian symbolism.

Of course it is impossible to know if Crane had this Christian symbolism in mind when he wrote the novel. In your own opinion, is the evidence strong enough to support this position, or do you consider it far-fetched?

5. **Theme.** Twice — at the end of Chapter VIII and in Chapter X — Henry flees from the tattered man. Why were the simple questions of the tattered man like "knife thrusts"? (page 428) How do these incidents touch a major theme of the novel?

6. An important paragraph (page 430) begins: "He searched about in his mind. . . ." Discuss the implications of this paragraph. What philosophical question is raised here? Is there any irony in Henry having this thought at this time?

7. Throughout these central chapters there is a pattern of alternating hope and despair, of rapidly changing fears and fantasies. Is this convincing? How typical is this of the inner life of a young person?

8. **Irony.** In Chapter XII, Henry is wounded. (page 435) Why is the way in which he is wounded ironic? Is this wound a "red badge of courage"?

9. Why, at the end of Chapter XIII, is Henry able to sink into a peaceful sleep? (page 444)

SECOND ENCOUNTER — CHAPTERS XIV–XXIII

1. In Chapter XV we read that the youth "felt immensely superior to his friend [the loud soldier]." (page 449) Why?

2. What is the metaphor in this quotation from Chapter XVII: "It was not well to drive men into final corners; at those moments they could all develop teeth and claws." (page 457) What definition of *courage* does this imply?

3. In the battle, what actions does Henry perform that turn him into a "hero"? What indications are there that his acts are not consciously reasoned out, but are blind and instinctive? Is what he does really heroic or courageous? Why or why not?

4. **Symbol.** Toward the end of Chapter XXIII, how do the battle flags become symbols for Henry and his fellow soldiers? (See especially pages 485–487.)

CONCLUSION — Chapter XXIV

1. During the novel we have seen Henry Fleming changing constantly. Often many conflicting points of view pass through his mind within the course of a few moments. What change comes to Henry in the last chapter? How does Crane suggest that this change is different from the others Henry has gone through? Is Crane's tone serious or ironic; that is, does he take this change in Henry seriously, or is Henry just fantasizing and rationalizing?
2. Crane writes, "He found that he could look back upon the brass and bombast of his earlier gospels and see them truly." (page 490) What were these earlier gospels? Why does the youth now despise them? What personal triumph has Henry won?

Interaction

1. **Plot.** A critic, J. C. Levenson, says about Crane: "War . . . gave him material he could . . . mold to his conception of outward *and* inner struggle." This remark suggests a great deal about the structure of *The Red Badge of Courage*. The novel moves forward on two lines of action. The first of these is concerned with the "outward struggle" — a war story, an adventure story. The second line of action is the psychological story of a youth achieving manhood; it concerns Henry Fleming's "inner struggle."

   In your opinion, what is the climax (the moment of greatest importance) of the novel's *outward* action? What is the climax of the *inner* action?

2. Discuss the topic "Concepts of Courage." In the course of your discussion, explain Stephen Crane's ideas about courage as they appear in *The Red Badge of Courage*. To avoid unsupported generalizations, make specific references to the novel. You may also wish to draw upon concepts of courage that appear in other selections in this book. Some of the selections which may be useful are: "John Colter's Race for Life" (page 36); "The Outcasts of Poker Flat" (page 44); "The Bride Comes to Yellow Sky" (page 68); "In Another Country" (page 504).

3. Discuss the following poem by Stephen Crane in relation to *The Red Badge of Courage*. What theme is treated in both the novel and the poem? In what way does the novel give a more rounded, more complete examination of the subject? What understanding

does Henry Fleming come to which is unknown to the youth in the poem?

> A youth in apparel that glittered
> Went to walk in a grim forest.
> There he met an assassin
> Attired all in garb of old days;
> He, scowling through the thickets,
> And dagger poised quivering,
> Rushed upon the youth.
> "Sir," said this latter,
> "I am enchanted, believe me,
> To die, thus,
> In this medieval fashion,
> According to the best legends;
> Ah, what joy!"
> Then he took the wound, smiling,
> And died, content.

4. When readers expressed surprise that Crane was not a veteran of the Civil War, he replied that he had learned the emotions of *The Red Badge of Courage* on the football field. How is this possible? What does Crane's remark tell us about the true meaning of his novel?

Three Poems: There Is a Gray Thing, A Man Said to the Universe, War Is Kind

---

Text pages 492–493

STEPHEN CRANE

Study Guide

1. Crane writes that only "those who meet death in the wilderness" see the gray thing face to face. What do the rest of us see?
2. Crane speaks of "the horror" of the thing and of its "wail of black laughter." What do you think the gray thing is?

3. "A Man Said to the Universe" is an ironic dialogue. What does the man seem to want? What is Crane's view of the relationship between man and the universe?
4. "War Is Kind" has a chorus, a repeated refrain, which emphasized Crane's irony. Each time the phrase is repeated the irony becomes more savage. What does Crane really think about war?
5. Crane pictures the wives, children, and mothers of soldiers weeping for the battle dead. And he pictures "a field where a thousand corpses lie." Why do the men fight, when the miseries of war are so clear?

Interaction

1. "There Is a Gray Thing" and "A Man Said to the Universe" might well have appeared in the section "Dark Voices in American Literature." What feeling about *indifference* is shared by Crane ("A Man Said to the Universe") and W. H. Auden (Musée des Beaux Arts," page 330)? In what way is the "gray thing" like the *night* in Frost's "Acquainted with the Night" (page 331)?
2. Judging from *The Red Badge of Courage* and "War Is Kind," discuss Stephen Crane's attitude toward war. In your discussion, consider Crane's feelings about the following:
   a) the ideological and political causes of wars
   b) the idea that death in battle is noble
   c) the "realities" of war
   d) the role of the individual soldier
   e) the end results of war
   You may also wish to discuss Crane's attitudes in a modern context, examining ways in which *The Red Badge* and "War Is Kind" correspond or do not correspond to attitudes and events today.

TRIALS OF MANHOOD

Americans respect courage and acts of manliness. We demand it of our leaders and heroes, and we reward it with fame. But what is it? What mysterious quality is contained in the words *manhood* and *manliness?* These words are the compliments we pay those individuals who show the persistence and quiet bravery of the early pioneers, or who show the dogged, lonely strength of an Abraham Lincoln in the bleakest days of the War between the States.

Some societies have rites or ceremonies of initiation that a young person must undergo before he can call himself a man. All such rites are concerned with testing the ability to undergo pain and hardship, both physical and mental, implying that the state of manhood is one of pain and hardship, a facing of problems and responsibilities. Our society has no such formal rites of initiation; our trials are more personal, less public, but no less real.

What are the problems and responsibilities that face the young person trying to cope with the demands and standards of the adult world? This question is the one dealt with in this section. What is manhood? It is certainly a difficult state to define and one that can cover a wide range of ages. Some of the characters in this section include grown men, a soldier, a teen-age girl, and a small boy. The elusive quality that seems to unite all these people is their courage in recognizing the weaknesses and conflicts within themselves and their attempt to overcome them. Manhood also implies a sense of personal integrity and worth that must not be compromised no matter what.

A Summer's Reading

Text pages 496–503

BERNARD MALAMUD *born:* 1914

Bernard Malamud grew up in Brooklyn, where his parents — Jewish immigrants from Russia — owned a neighborhood grocery store. In many of his stories and novels Malamud captures the bleakness, the humor, the humanity, and the dialects of his Brooklyn home. But Malamud's style and settings have varied greatly: *The Natural* is a fantasy about a great baseball hero; *The Fixer*, based on actual events, is about a Jew's hideous tortures in a Russian prison; *A New Life* transplants a New Yorker to the West; and *Pictures of Fidelman* concerns an American artist in Italy. Malamud's "heroes" hardly seem heroic, at least at first. One of Malamud's most consistent themes is the way in which people change: the regeneration of ordinary, unheroic people. "To me writing must be true," Malamud once wrote; "it must have emotional depth; it must be imaginative. It must enflame, destroy, change the reader."

Comment

Along with the theme of suffering, one finds in Malamud the theme of the meaningful life, which is the antithesis of the "unlived life," against which his characters are always contending.

— PHILIP RAHV: A Malamud Reader

Study Guide

1. What is the central decision George is faced with in this story? It is something much deeper than whether he will or will not read books.
2. Although the story has relatively little physical action, there is a constant tension of opposing forces pulling George in two different directions, toward two different futures — a man's and a boy's. What things in the story symbolize these opposing forces? What two places hold the most attraction for him?
3. It is not a single motive but rather a complex set of motives which drives George to the library. What do you think these motives are?

Interaction

Philip Rahv (see **Comment**) finds throughout Malamud's work the "theme of the meaningful life, which is the anthithesis of the 'unlived life.'" How does this theme apply to George's experience in "A Summer's Reading"?

In Another Country

Text pages 504–509

Ernest Hemingway 1899–1961

Literary critics are endlessly reminding us that we must not confuse a writer's biography with his works. In Hemingway's case this is an important distinction to make, but Hemingway made it difficult for us to do. When he was Hemingway the Writer — that is, when he was writing at his best — he was disciplined, subtle, and profoundly engaged with the ethical and moral implications of the smallest human actions. When he was Hemingway the Man — the public role he played out in bullrings, bars, and battlefields — he sometimes appeared to be crude, bullying, and insensitive. In fact, Hemingway was a highly educated man, a most sensitive man; like many artists he felt the need to protect his inner self from the public. The bragging, adventuring, brawling Hemingway was the defense he erected. But Hemingway will be remembered as an artist long after he is forgotten as an adventurer.

Hemingway's heroes did more or less the same things that their author did. They grew up in the Midwest, fought and were wounded in the First World War (the background for "In Another Country"). They hunted big game in Africa, fished for marlin off Cuba, took part in the Civil War in Spain. They sought out situations in which men were tested by being given the opportunity to show "grace under pressure."

It was as a young journalist living in Paris in the 1920's that Ernest Hemingway began to write seriously and to shape the distinctive prose style for which he became famous. The style was an athletic one; that is, it attempted to be powerful and direct, to perform accurate feats of speed and grace in the most economical way. There was an attempt to convey in prose the exact patterns and shadings of sensation and feeling experienced by his characters. Sometimes this prose was so simple that it almost sounded as if it were written for a children's book. Only its precision saved it from being banal. The sentences were short; the words were very plain and often were repeated. Listen to the first two sentences of "In Another Country" — they exemplify the Hemingway style. Notice that most of the words have only one syllable:

> In the fall the war was always there, but we did not go to it any more. It was cold in the fall in Milan and the dark came very early.

At first Hemingway concentrated on writing short stories, among the most famous of which are "Big Two-Hearted River," "The Killers," and "The Snows of Kilimanjaro." After sharpening his style on shorter fiction, he turned to the novel. Among his best-known novels are *A Farewell to Arms* (about the First World War), *The Sun Also Rises* (about the "lost generation" of exiles living in Spain and Paris in the twenties), and *For Whom the Bell Tolls* (about the Spanish Civil War). During and following the Second World War there was a long period in which he published almost nothing. Then in 1952 he won great popular and critical acclaim for his short novel about an aging fisherman's last "battle for life," *The Old Man and the Sea*. In 1954 he was awarded the Nobel Prize. During his last years Hemingway found himself much like the aging fisherman he wrote about in that book: he was no longer able to perform the one task that gave his life meaning. His mind was no longer able to produce the kind of writing that pleased him. He committed suicide at his hunting lodge in Idaho in 1961.

Comments

Mr. Hemingway is remarkably successful in suggesting moral values by a series of simple statements.   — EDMUND WILSON

But the things that Hemingway's style most suggests are the very things that he has been trying also to say directly and outright. His style is as eloquent of his content as the content itself; the style is a large part of the content. The strictly disciplined controls which he has exerted over his hero and his "bad nerves" are precise parallels to the strictly disciplined sentences he writes. Understatement, abbreviated statement, and lack of statement reflect without the slightest distortion the rigid restraint which the man feels he must practice if he is to survive. The "mindlessness" of the style is the result of a need to "stop thinking," and is the purest reflection of that need. The intense simplicity of the prose is a means by which the man says, Things must be *made* simple, or I am lost, in a way you'll never be.   — PHILIP YOUNG: Hemingway

Study Guide

1. How do the season and the landscape, so carefully presented in the first paragraph, reflect the mood and meaning of the whole story?

2. In what ways are the soldiers in the hospital like the fox, deer, and game birds described in the opening paragraph?
3. The story is certainly a bleak one. Is there any ray of hope at all for any of the characters?
4. Consider the title. In what sense is the narrator "in another country"? In what sense are all of the soldiers, even the Italians, "in another country"?
5. In Hemingway's world the characters often seem to accept bad luck, misfortune, and loss as ordinary parts of life. The important thing is the way they behave in the face of tragic circumstances. How do the wounded soldiers in this story accept their misfortune? Do they ever complain? What code of behavior does the major have?
6. What difference between the major and the American narrator is suggested by the following dialogue? (page 508)

> "He should not place himself in a position to lose. He should find things he cannot lose."
> He spoke very angrily and bitterly, and looked straight ahead while he talked.
> "But why should he necessarily lose it?"
> "He'll lose it," the major said.

7. What are the implications of the third sentence from the end: "I do not know where the doctor got them [the photographs]"?
8. What is tragic about the major's statement, "I am utterly unable to resign myself" — in light of the major's own philosophy?
9. At the end of the story the major refuses to look at the photographs; he stares out the window at the landscape, which (although it is not again described) we know is a wintry one. If the major has no real faith in "the machines," why is he going on with the treatments? What code of life does this suggest?

Interaction

1. What attitude toward war do you find in this story?
2. Sometimes people object to literature as bleak and tragic as this story by Hemingway. Their argument often runs like this: Life is so full of evil and misery that there is no reason to read about it. They claim that when they read they want to be "entertained," not "depressed." What defense can you make for the value of a story like "In Another Country"?

Two Soldiers

Text pages 510–525

WILLIAM FAULKNER 1897–1962

Like Hemingway, William Faulkner often presented himself as a man who was less well educated and less well read than in fact he was. For most of his life he lived in Oxford, Mississippi, which became in his stories Jefferson, the county seat of the legendary region about which he wrote his greatest books. Since most of his novels were not popular until long after he wrote them, he earned little from his writings. Occasionally he would go to Hollywood, where he earned a living by writing screenplays. But he always returned to the privacy he found in Mississippi. He did not like to talk about his work, and in Oxford he could better avoid the "literary" world and the professors and journalists who wanted to interview him. Once two of his admirers traveled to Oxford to meet him. They found Faulkner fishing. All the men could think to say was, "Catch anything?" Faulkner said no, he hadn't. Suddenly the two visitors understood that they were trespassing upon a private world. With no further conversation they left.

For years Faulkner spun out an epic about the American South, but it is an epic with universal as well as local application. In Faulkner's South the past always presses hard upon the present. His characters bear the full weight of history, both the glories and the sins of their ancestors. To a large extent he admired the aristocratic, rural, prewar South; but he saw the ideals of his grandfather's and great-grandfather's generations crumbling before the onslaught of a new breed of mean-minded, greedy businessmen. In his great novels — though they are laced with comedy — there is a brooding atmosphere as tragic fate is transferred from generation to generation.

Faulkner's work is often difficult, filled with obscure symbolism and expressed in a rhetorical prose (unlike Hemingway's spare expression) which contains some of the longest sentences ever written in English.

Among Faulkner's most famous novels and stories — those in which he creates his mythical Yoknapatawpha County — are *The Sound and the Fury; Sartoris; Light in August; Absolom, Absolom!; Go Down, Moses and Other Stories* (which includes the classic story "The Bear"); and *Intruder in the Dust.*

In his later years, when great fame finally came to him (he won the Nobel Prize in 1950), Faulkner became more of a public figure. He began to make direct statements about his own work, about racial problems, and about the condition of mankind in an atomic world. During his last years he lived in Charlottesville, Virginia, where he was writer in residence at the University. He died in Oxford, July 7, 1962.

Comment

The constant ethical center of Faulkner's work is to be found in the glorification of human effort and human endurance. . . . The point is that they are found most often in people who are outside the stream of the dominant world. . . . Faulkner's world is full of "good people."　　　— ROBERT PENN WARREN: Selected Essays

Study Guide

1. Faulkner tells his story from the point of view of a nine-year-old boy. Because of his age, the narrator is innocent and inexperienced in many ways. What things that puzzle, frighten, or pain him does the reader understand more fully? How would the story change if Pete were the narrator and the story were told from his point of view? That is, what incidents would have to be omitted or changed?
2. The characterization of the young boy is almost entirely by indirect means, by implication. List three speeches or actions that you feel are important to an understanding of the boy. Does he seem to be intelligent? Cite evidence to support your answer.
3. What kind of relationship does the young boy have with his brother Pete at the beginning? How do the two farewells between the brothers tell of a change in this relationship? (See pages 515 and 523.)
4. How does the narrator react to the people he meets on his trip? How do the adults react to him? Do they treat him with humor and condescension as you might expect in a situation with a boy running away from home? Do their reactions imply anything about the boy?
5. Language. One of the ways in which Faulkner makes his narrator come alive for us is by using language that the narrator would actually use. A good example is "Me and Pete" instead of the more

conventionally correct "Pete and I." What other words and phrases express the age and background of the narrator?

6. In one sense, the boy comes through his trial of manhood unsuccessfully: he does not achieve his goal of joining Pete in the Army, because he is a child. But the war and Pete's leaving have brought the boy into the adult world. What adult responsibilities face him when he returns home? How do you think he will handle them?

Interaction

1. Much American literature uses dialect. Which stories, plays, and poems in IDEAS AND PATTERNS IN LITERATURE use one or more levels of speech or the local dialects of Americans?

2. The journey away from home is an important part of many stories about trials of manhood. As in *Old Times on the Mississippi,* the journey presents the main character with new experiences and problems, and often these mature him. How does the boy's journey in "Two Soldiers" change him?

Sixteen

Text pages 526–533

JESSAMYN WEST   *born:* 1907

Jessamyn West began writing while convalescing from an illness. One of her most popular books, *The Friendly Persuasion,* is based on her own Quaker upbringing, though it is set during the Civil War. "Sixteen" is taken from another popular book, *Cress Delahanty,* a collection of stories about a teen-age girl.

Study Guide

1. The story begins with a description of a "cold" window and a "bleak" darkening grove. Even though it is morning, the smoke from the smudge pots creates darkness and adds to the mood of impending death. Contrast this scene with the scene between Cress and Edwin in the groves at college.

2. Cress has unbounded enthusiasm for nature; she tells Edwin, for example, "No one in the world loves the meadow lark's song the

way I do!" (page 528) At the same time, Cress has no use for things outside her romantic world. Of the aged gardener, she says, "He's old. . . . He doesn't exist." (page 529) What change has taken place in Cress at the end of the story?

3. The change occurs because of something seemingly very minor — a bunch of flowers. What do the flowers represent to Cress? to her grandfather?

4. What is the meaning of the last sentence? Was Edwin right, and does the grandfather do something for Cress? Explain.

Interaction

1. Each of the selections in the section so far has emphasized the influence of other people, or one individual, on the growth of a young person. Mr. Cattanzara, the Major, Pete, and Cress's grandfather make a lasting impression on the main characters of the stories. Write a short composition about someone who has influenced you.

2. Many stories about the trials of manhood are "success stories": for example, the knight who rescues the damsel from the dragon and the poor boy who goes from rags to riches and romance. A more sophisticated version of the "success story" is Charles Dickens's *Great Expectations*, in which a poor orphan becomes a gentleman of means.

   Do the leading characters of Malamud's, Hemingway's, Faulkner's, and West's stories gain any *material* advantages, as do those of the "success stories"? Would you say that the characters in this unit are failures rather than "successes"? Defend your answer with specific references to the selections.

Requiem for a Heavyweight

Text pages 534–585

ROD SERLING   *born:* 1924

Rod Serling was introduced to the fight arena as a paratrooper in World War II. More than a decade later he drew on his amateur boxing experiences for *Requiem*. With teleplays like *Requiem*, performed on October 11, 1956, Serling became one of the first television writers to win the respect of the video audience and critics. Serling created more than a hundred plays for television, many of which have been brought back again and again by popular demand.

In his teleplays, Serling usually explored some timely social or moral issue; for example, *Patterns* discusses power struggles in big business; *The Rank and File*, corruption in labor unions; and *The Town Has Turned to Dust*, lynch mobs. Eventually Serling was hampered by censorship from sponsors and television executives. He turned to fantasy, creating *The Twilight Zone*, which disguised his social and moral themes as science fiction. Stories from *The Twilight Zone* has been published in book form and are occasionally replayed on television.

Study Guide

1. One of the patterns shared by literature of many ages and countries is the pattern of romance. You'll recognize it in many fairy tales: a handsome young prince goes on a quest to win fame and fortune for himself by rescuing a beautiful maiden. On the way he overcomes dragons or monsters with the help of a companion: an old and kind wise man, or a stupid and clumsy servant. They generally meet and outwit an evil witch or evil magician.

   Although this myth seems very remote from our present plastic and atomic age, the narrative pattern of the quest or search, the obstacles to be overcome, and the successful rescue of a beautiful girl is a recurring one even now. One way to add to your understanding and enjoyment of literature is to observe ways in which individual writers vary the pattern.

   What characters and events in this play reflect those of the older romances? Who might correspond to the hero on a quest? to the companion? to the evil witch or magician? Consider the ways Serling has varied the pattern. For example, does the hero rescue the beautiful maiden? or does she rescue him?

2. The nature of a play, especially one written for television, requires that the characters be developed with economy and precision. Unlike the novel or short story, the drama requires that characters be presented solely through dialogue and action. What are the general character attributes of Mountain, Maish, and Army?

3. After the opening description of a harsh, bleak scene, attention is immediately focused upon Mountain and his deep, bleeding

cuts and bruises sustained in the fight. Give further examples of the way in which the author realistically re-creates the brutality of the world of prizefighting through his use of both setting and dialogue.

4. Army and Mountain differ significantly in their views of the world and of other characters, especially Maish. Army has deeper insight into Maish in contrast to Mountain's naive trust. Give specific examples of the difference in their views of Maish and also of the way in which Army's deeper insight provides the audience with new and necessary information.

5. What is your reaction to the character of Maish? Does he fit easily into a category or does he remain somewhat ambiguous? Consider his generally selfish and unfeeling attitude toward Mountain and the ending of his career. His remarks sometimes are nearly brutal. Yet when Mountain asks Maish not to make him wrestle, Maish appears to be genuinely suffering for what he is doing. What type of attitudes prevalent today might Maish's actions represent? At what points in the play do you sympathize with Maish? In what ways is he a more complex character than either Mountain or Army?

6. What are the main reasons that Mountain rebels against the whole idea of wearing a costume? Mountain is sensitive, proud, and honorable, but the tactlessness and unintentional cruelty of other people — especially women — have made him think of himself as a freak. What occurs in the play to alter this opinion of himself? How does his new opinion of himself influence his decision not to wrestle?

7. Like Army, Grace is sympathetic, understanding, and perceptive. How is her background different from Mountain's? Why does she try to help Mountain at first? Do you think it is believable that she would fall in love with Mountain? Explain.

8. Among other things, Serling is dealing with values. Show how attitudes toward money are pitted against basic human and humane values in the play.

9. A *requiem* is a hymn for the dead. A good example of a requiem is Melville's "Shiloh." (page 261) In what sense is the word *requiem* used in Serling's title? Why is the end of his boxing career a beginning for Mountain?

10. The action and the title of the play focus upon the ending of Mountain's career. Do you think the inability to fight any longer caused Mountain as much suffering as his knowledge of the way

in which Maish betrayed him? Give reasons to support your opinion.

Interaction

1. Suppose you were casting a movie or a new television version of this play. What actors and actresses would you cast in the major roles?
2. One of the most significant camera directions, both in teleplays and in movies, is the close-up. Often in a close-up the entire screen is filled with the image of one thing — an actor's face, for instance. The close-up is a device used for emphasis, and therefore it must be used only at particular moments. Look at the close-up directions on pages 543, 547, 552, and 570. Each one indicates that the image on the television screen, rather than words, will communicate something important. What do each of the close-ups communicate?
3. At the time *Requiem for a Heavyweight* was written, the television audience, sponsors, and network executives demanded certain things of a teleplay. For example, the language had to be inoffensive, even though men in the world of boxing might not, in real life, be very careful in speaking. Another demand was that a story have a love interest (a demand that has held true for audiences in all times and countries). Still another demand was that the ending be uplifting, if not perfectly happy. Rod Serling's teleplay fulfills each of these demands. Consider the realism or lack of realism, effectiveness or ineffectiveness of each of the following:
    a) Mountain's final words to Maish (pages 578–579)
    b) the romance between Mountain and Grace
    c) the last scene (page 585)
    Do any of these features of the teleplay strike you as sentimenal or old-fashioned? Why or why not?
4. The movie version of *Requiem for a Heavyweight* has a different ending from the ending in the teleplay. The last scene in the movie shows Mountain in the wrestling ring, costumed, and sacrificing his pride and integrity for Maish's sake. Do you think the ending of the movie version is more believable than the ending of the teleplay? What traits in Mountain would make this self-sacrifice believable? What traits in Mountain would make it unbelievable?

The Making of a Writer's Mind

Text pages 586–593

RALPH ELLISON   *born:* 1914

There are very few cases in which the publication of only one novel makes a writer as important as *Invisible Man* made Ralph Ellison. When it appeared in 1952 it won the National Book Award. Thirteen years later a poll of two hundred editors, authors, and critics named *Invisible Man* the most significant addition to American literature in twenty years.

Ellison was born in Oklahoma. He started out to become a classical musician, later turned to jazz. Since the publication of *Invisible Man* he has also published *Shadow and Act*, a collection of essays from which "The Making of a Writer's Mind" is taken. He has taught at many American universities.

Although Ellison writes mostly about the experience of being a Negro in America, his concerns are not limited to racial problems. The broader theme of *Invisible Man* and his other writings is the struggle of man to find an identity for himself and to preserve his individuality.

Comment

Fully aware of the limitations placed upon the Negro in America, Ellison has nevertheless chosen to emphasize those positive elements in Negro life that have helped to keep American culture rich and varied. "Hidden Name and Complex Fate" . . . clearly illustrates Ellison's central ideas: his affinity to Emersonian idealism and his insistence that we cherish those human differences that make being an American a complex fate.

— JAMES A. EMMANUAL *and* THEODORE L. GROSS: Dark Symphony

Study Guide

1. The development of sensitivity and imagination, Ellison shows, was important in making him a writer. How did his name and his games with the lens help to stimulate his imagination? In what ways was the young Ellison sensitive to his surroundings?
2. Ellison does not refer to just Oklahoma City, but to *Negro* Oklahoma City; not just to his community, but to the *Negro* commu-

nity. One reason he does this is to emphasize the cultural influences on him, influences which sprang specifically from the Negro culture. What were some of these influences? The frequent references to the Negro community indicate that Ellison grew up in a society which was in many ways alienated from the rest of American society. Is there any indication that Ellison also felt alienated from his own society, as the other young people in this section on "Trials of Manhood" do? Or does he identify closely with his community?

3. Ellison often uses contrast in his essay. He places opposites side by side in an illuminating way. For example, he says that he read hate literature as well as the Harvard Classics. What other examples of contrast do you find in the essay? What do you think is Ellison's purpose in using contrasts?

4. In the last sentence Ellison speaks of his "sense of life." How would you describe his "sense of life"?

Interaction

1. Although Ellison shares two out of three names with Ralph Waldo Emerson, their writings seem to have little in common. What are some of the differences in their writing? (See pages 343–351 for Emerson's writings.) Do you find any similarities?

2. Unlike the others you've read about in this section, Ellison had to face no *one* specific "trial of manhood." However, Ellison does tell us here about the formative period of his life and some of the obstacles he had to overcome. What were some of these obstacles?

3. Consider the "making" of your own mind as Ellison has done in this essay. What influences — names, communities, books, music, ways of speech, specific experiences — have made you the person that you are? The more specific you make your answer the more revealing and interesting it will be. Notice that Ellison is always specific: he does not stop at telling the reader that nature has influenced him — he tells us exactly what kinds of nature surrounded him: ". . . spring floods and blizzards; catalpa worms and jack rabbits; honeysuckle and snapdragons (which smelled like old cigar butts); by sunflowers and hollyhocks. . . ."

Trials of Manhood: Summing Up

1. One of the things the selections in this section all have in common is that they look at a young person who in some ways is an outsider. Although none of them is rebelling against his society, each is alienated from it. How is each of the following, at least in part, alienated from his society?
   a) George Stoyonovich in "A Summer's Reading"
   b) the narrator of "In Another Country"
   c) the young boy in "Two Soldiers"
   d) Mountain McClintock in *Requiem for a Heavyweight*
   e) Ralph Ellison in "The Making of a Writer's Mind"
   Which ones come to a compromise which enables them to rejoin society? Which ones remain outsiders?
   Some people believe that alienation among American youth is "wider, deeper, and more diffuse than at any previous time in our history. It affects the rich and the poor, the college student and the drop-out, the urban and the rural youngster." To what extent, in your opinion, is alienation a problem among young people today?

2. "Trials of Manhood" is a significant theme in the literature of America as well as that of other countries. In addition to the selections in this unit, *Old Times on the Mississippi*, "Young Goodman Brown," and *The Red Badge of Courage* also focus on a young person's entry into adulthood. Why do you think this theme has concerned so many writers?

THE INDIVIDUAL AND SOCIETY

In 1958 William Faulkner was interviewed by a group of students at the University of Virginia. The questions turned to individualism:

Q. Most of your characters are certainly highly individualized human beings. Do you have any particular ideas on the so-called trend toward conformity, the loss of individualization in our current society?

A. Yes, I have very definite ideas about that, and if I ever become a preacher, it will be to preach against man, individual man, relinquishing into groups, any group. I'm against belonging to anything. Of course, when I was young I belonged to young people's fraternities and things like that, but now I don't want to belong to anything except the human race.

Q. Why is that?

A. I think that there's too much pressure to make people conform and I think that one man may be first-rate but if you get one man and two second-rate men together, then he's not going to be first-rate any longer, because the voice of that majority will be a second-rate voice, the behavior of that majority will be second-rate. And I think that a second-rate man to save himself at least won't be third-rate, but no second-rate man is going to become first-rate just by joining one or two more first-rate people.

Q. Can you go further and say how you rate people like that — first and second-rate?

A. Well sir, that would be a little difficult and maybe a little trite. I would say that a first-rate man is one — is a man that did the best he could with what talents he had to make something which wasn't here yesterday. And also to — that never hurt an inferior, never harmed the weak, practiced honesty and courtesy, and tried to be as brave as he wanted to be whether he always was that brave or not. I think that a man that held to those tenets wouldn't get very far if he were involved in a group of people that had relinquished their individualities to some one voice which would — could control their behavior.

A Different Drummer

Text pages 597–600

HENRY DAVID THOREAU 1817–1862

A legend has grown up about Thoreau's famous night in jail, a legend which has some basis in fact and which tells a great deal about the kind of man Thoreau was. Thoreau went to jail for refusing to pay his poll tax; he refused to pay it as a protest against the United States's entry into the Mexican War. According to the legend, Emerson visited Thoreau in jail: "Henry, what are you doing in there?" Thoreau replied, "Ralph, what are you doing out there?" This dialogue illustrates Thoreau's philosophy that a man can and should act on his convictions. It was Emerson who wrote, "Things are in the saddle and ride men." But it was Thoreau who turned his back on "things" and went to live in the woods.

Thoreau was born in Concord, Massachusetts, where he lived for most of his life. As a student at Harvard he began keeping a journal, a habit that was to lead to his great works. After college Thoreau was faced with the workaday world. He was handy around his family's house and pencil shop but spent most of his time reading and walking in the woods. He tried schoolteaching but was fired for refusing to flog the pupils. While Thoreau was looking for something to do with his life, Emerson — fourteen years his senior — opened the doors of his home and invited Thoreau's company, friendship, and ideas.

It was this friendship that helped Thoreau fulfill his promise. Emerson encouraged Thoreau's writing. He helped Thoreau look for ways to make a living and continued to support him when he failed. At one time Thoreau went to New York, with a hearty recommendation from Emerson, to work for the famous journalist and abolitionist, Horace Greeley. But, Thoreau observed, "I carry Concord ground in my boots and in my hat." Soon he was back in Concord, twenty-six years old and still at loose ends.

Then Emerson offered his friend a lot on Walden Pond. There he could work and study as he pleased without becoming one of the "mass of men" who, Thoreau felt, lead "lives of quiet desperation." "I went to the woods," Thoreau wrote in *Walden*, "because I wished to live deliberately, to front only the essential facts of life, and see if I could not learn what it had to teach."

After two years, two months, and two days, Thoreau returned to Concord. He brought with him journals filled with his mystical and practical observations of nature; with the help of these journals he fashioned *Walden*. The journals also contained Thoreau's thoughts on the individual's responsibility when his government is unjust and immoral. These ideas became "Civil Disobedience," a work that was later to influence such men as Mahatma Ghandi and Martin Luther King, Jr. These ideas also spurred Thoreau's protests against the Fugitive Slave Law, his support of John Brown, and his sojourn in jail. (Thoreau was released from jail the next day after an anonymous citizen paid his tax.)

Thoreau never was a "success" in the usual sense of that word. For many years, even after the publication of *Walden* in 1854, he was barely noticed outside of Concord. In a more important sense, however, Thoreau was a success. The quality of his life (and wit) can be seen in a conversation that took place as he was dying. His aunt asked him if he had made his peace with God. Thoreau replied, "Why, Aunt, I didn't know we had ever quarreled!"

Comments

Mr. Thoreau dined with us yesterday. He is a singular character — a young man with much of wild original stuff still remaining in him; and so far as he is sophisticated, it is in a way and method of his own. He is as ugly as sin, long-nosed, queer-mouthed, and with uncouth and somewhat rustic, although courteous manners, corresponding very well with such an exterior. But his ugliness is of an honest and agreeable fashion, and becomes him much better than beauty. He was educated, I believe at Cambridge, and formerly kept school in this town; but for two or three years back, he has repudiated all regular modes of getting a living, and seems inclined to lead a sort of Indian life among civilized men — an Indian life, I mean, as respects the absence of any systematic effort for a livelihood. He has been for sometime an inmate of Mr. Emerson's family; and, in requital, he labors in the garden, and performs such other offices as may suit him — being entertained by Mr. Emerson for the sake of what true manhood there is in him. Mr. Thoreau is a keen and delicate observer of nature — a genuine observer, which, I suspect, is almost as rare a character as even an original poet; and Nature, in return for his love, seems to adopt him as her special child, and shows him secrets which few others are allowed to witness. He is familiar with beast, fish, fowl, and reptile, and has strange stories to tell of his adventures, and friendly passages with these lower brethren of mortality. . . . With all this he has more than a tincture of literature — a deep and true taste for poetry, especially the elder poets. . . . On the whole I find him a healthy and wholesome man to know.   — NATHANIEL HAWTHORNE: Notebooks

Thoreau is as near the Emersonian concept of Man Thinking as any writer of his or our time. The whole man stands back of the effort. What he sought was wholly sought. What he realized was wholly realized. When he says injunctively, "We must *live* all our *life*," he is reporting the singleness of purpose in his own effort. Because his writings embody acts of life, one must first see and feel what he lived in order to share his experience.

    — REGINALD L. COOK: Passage to Walden

Study Guide

1. Like Hawthorne and Emerson, Thoreau believed that the spiritual world reveals itself in the natural world. Because of this belief, Thoreau used metaphors from nature and daily life to express his philosophy. What ideas does Thoreau express in the following metaphors?

    a) "I did not wish to take a cabin passage, but rather to go before the mast and on the deck of the world, for there I could best see the moonlight amid the mountains." (page 598)

    b) "If a man does not keep pace with his companions, perhaps it is because he hears a different drummer. Let him step to the music which he hears, however measured or far away." (page 598)

    c) "The setting sun is reflected from the windows of the almshouse as brightly as from the rich man's abode." (page 599)

    Discuss other metaphors Thoreau uses to express his philosophy.

2. Thoreau wrote:

I learned this, at least, by my experiment; that if one advances confidently in the direction of his dreams, and endeavors to live the life which he has imagined, he will meet with a success unexpected in common hours. He will put some things behind, will pass an invisible boundary; new, universal, and more liberal laws will begin to establish themselves around and within him.

What does Thoreau mean by "success"? How does his definition differ from society's usual definitions? What two ways of life does the "invisible boundary" separate?
3. What criticism does Thoreau make of society in this essay? What hope does he hold out for mankind?
4. James Russell Lowell said of Thoreau: "He took nature as the mountain path to an ideal world." What are some of the aspects of Thoreau's "ideal world"? What does Thoreau believe should be a person's goals in life?

Interaction

1. What distinction can you make between Thoreau's defiance of society and praise of the individual and many of the present-day rioters and lawbreakers? Do they both seem to be arguing from the same position, or is there an important difference? Suppose someone offered to supply Thoreau with drugs that would enable him to grasp the realms of his "infinite mind," for the pursuit of happiness. What might Thoreau's reaction be?
2. What does Thoreau mean when he refers to "the dead dry life of society"? What do you consider is the "dead dry life" of modern society? Norman Mailer, a contemporary writer, states that the American writer has lost the "belief in the efficacy of attacking his society." What attacks on society are being made today? Do you agree that such attacks are useless? Explain your answer.

Letter to My Nephew

Text pages 601–605

JAMES BALDWIN born: 1924

Novelist, essayist, and playwright, James Baldwin began his career as a preacher in Harlem's storefront churches. His first novel, Go Tell It On The Mountain (1953) and his Notes of a Native Son won applause from critics, who praised Baldwin's eloquence and outspokenness. But it wasn't until 1961, with the publication of Nobody Knows My Name, that Baldwin began to be read widely by the general public. Baldwin then became something of a national figure, frequently appearing on television to speak out on national issues.

Study Guide

1. This essay uses many surprising and provocative expressions. Paying particular attention to the italicized words, explain Baldwin's meaning in these statements:

   a) ". . . most of them do not yet *really know that you exist*." (page 603)

   b) "This *innocent* country set you down in a ghetto in which, in fact, it *intended that you should perish*." (page 603)

   c) "There is no reason for you to try to become like white people, and there is no basis whatever for their *impertinent* assumption that *they* must accept *you*." (page 604)

2. What does Baldwin feel is the attitude that destroyed his father? What attitude does he want his nephew to have toward himself? toward white people?

3. Baldwin refers to white men as "your lost, younger brothers." He believes that prejudice keeps the white man enslaved. How does he feel the black man can set the white man free? Why do you think he feels that this is the *black* man's, and not the *white* man's, responsibility?

Interaction

1. With which of the following statements would Baldwin be most likely to agree? Defend your choice with references to his essay.

   a) Before the individual can take an active part in improving society, he must find the life that is best for himself.

   b) The individual must reject his fellow men when they insist on conformity.

   c) In order to achieve his individual ideals, a man must see to it that his society lives up to its ideals.

   With which of these statements would Thoreau be most likely to agree?

2. How does Baldwin's letter compare in style, tone, and purpose with Franklin's letter to Priestley (page 340)?

3. Reactions to Baldwin's essay span the spectrum from a fear that what he says is too fiery to a feeling that it is not fiery enough. He overturns many widely held assumptions in this essay. For example, he writes that the black man has to learn to accept the white man and that the black man must set the white man free, thus reversing some of the clichés about race relations in this country. There is some anger, some bitterness in the tone, but

the word stressed is *love:* "You must accept them and accept them with love"; ". . . we, with love, shall force our brothers to see themselves as they are." (page 604)

What is your personal reaction to this essay? Refer both to some of its specific ideas and to its central theme.

The Sculptor's Funeral

Text pages 606–620

WILLA CATHER   1876–1947

Red Cloud, Nebraska, the town in which Willa Cather was raised, was a frontier town still being settled by pioneers. After graduating from college, Miss Cather taught in high school, worked as a reporter and editor in New York, and traveled in America and Europe. She drew upon her intimate knowledge of the prairie country for much of her best fiction: *Death Comes for the Archbishop, My Antonia,* and *O Pioneers!* Like "The Sculptor's Funeral," these novels reveal the author's characteristic reserved tone and the recurring theme of the artistic or highly sensitive person in a materialistic society.

Comment

Yet her favorite theme persists throughout: the conflict of the superior individual with an unworthy society. And since this society is her version of the world in which she has lived — of the West primarily, and incidentally of the United States — it may be taken to embody implicitly her conception of American life. Her view is that the pioneers in general were folk largely endowed with creative power and imagination, but that the second generation, except for a few artists who have inherited the spirit of the fathers, has degenerated and succumbed to the tyranny of ease and money and things. Usually she sets off society against the background of natural grandeur. I cannot agree . . . that she has few revenges to take on her environment. On the contrary, her scarification of it, repeated again and again, is as vitriolic as that of any contemporary. The American community, whether family or town or neighborhood, is always the villain of the piece. It is the foe of life; it is worse than sterile — deadly, poisonous, adverse to human growth, hostile to every humane quality. She shows us communities of people who are little and petty but withal complacent and self-satisfied, who are intolerant and contemptuous of what differs from themselves, who are tightly bound by conventionality — not the sort that springs from free, deliberate approval of conventions, but the sort that has its source in cowardice, stupidity, or indolence — of people who hate whatever does not jibe with their twopenny ha'penny aims, who hate everything genuine and human — genuine thought, or religion, or righteousness, or beauty — everything that means being genuinely alive, everything that shows true mind or feeling or imagination. In consequence, the living individual is not only of necessity isolated and cut off from sustaining human relationships, but thwarted and frustrated so far as possible.

— T. K. WHIPPLE: Willa Catha

Study Guide

1. **Tone.** Which character or characters do you think represent Willa Cather's attitude toward the sculptor's family and town? How would you describe this attitude?
2. **Theme.** Willa Cather writes: "All this raw, biting ugliness had been the portion of the man whose mind was to become an exhaustless gallery of beautiful impressions. . . ." (page 614) How did Harvey rise above the "raw, biting ugliness" of Sand City?
3. **Point of view.** Once the train arrives, the story is told from the point of view of the sculptor's young friend from Boston. What is Steavens like — did he strike you as a conceited snob? (Remember he found the grieving mother repulsive; he viewed Jim Laird as a "sooty . . . lump of potter's clay.") Or did his feelings about the townspeople correspond to yours?
4. **Characterization.**
    a) The townspeople. What are the values that seem to preside over this community? In what respect is the name of the town (Sand City) appropriate?
    b) Mrs. Merrick (the sculptor's mother). How does she impress Steavens? ("She filled the room; the men were obliterated, seemed tossed about like twigs in an angry water." page 610) What seems to have been her effect upon the various members of her family?

c) Harvey Merrick. What do the townspeople remember most about Harvey? Two questions are raised about Harvey but are not answered directly. (1) Why did he want to come home to be buried? (2) What secret ("something precious and holy") does Harvey seem to be guarding even in death? Reread the paragraph about the bas-relief beginning "Once when Merrick returned from a visit home. . . ." (page 613) What does the butterfly seem to symbolize?

d) Jim Laird. What was the basis of the close relationship between Jim and Harvey? Why did Jim drink?

Interaction

1. For many writers the small town retains associations of wholesome morality, of uncomplicated social patterns, and of continuity from generation to generation. For instance, the picture of small town life in *Our Town*, which you will read in the next section, is positive. Describe Willa Cather's picture of small-town life. What conflicts between the individual and small-town society does she describe? What do you think are some of the advantages and disadvantages of living in a small town?

2. The critic Howard Mumford Jones has written that the theme of "The Sculptor's Funeral" is the "conflict between beauty and reality." Do you agree? Why or why not? Jones goes on to say, "Merrick's death is immaterial; what matters is Merrick's life, dedicated to self-fulfillment." What is Willa Cather's idea of "self-fulfillment"? What does her idea have in common with Thoreau's (page 597) and Emerson's? (page 343)

Flowers for Algernon

Text pages 621–650

DANIEL KEYES   born: 1927

Flowers for Algernon has appeared as a television drama, and as a science-fiction story in several languages. It was later expanded into a longer version and, still later, made into a movie, *Charly*. Keyes's career also includes work as an English teacher, an editor, a merchant seaman, and a photographer. He is now on the faculty of Ohio State University.

Study Guide

1. By his diary structure ("progris riport") Keyes brings us close to the thoughts and feelings of a mentally retarded young man, a young man who works hard to learn more, but does not have the mental ability to do so. What do you think of Charlie as a person? Does your attitude toward him change after his operation? Why or why not?

2. How do people treat the retarded Charlie? How do they treat the genius? What different attitudes toward intelligence does Keyes show in this story?

3. Why does Charlie want to be "smart"? (page 625)

4. What in Charlie's journal is the first indication that he has advanced beyond mere memorization of facts? Why is he deeply affected by *Robinson Crusoe*? (page 630)

5. What changes take place in Charlie's understanding of the world he lives in?

6. **Significant detail.** Many of the details of a short story are interesting because they develop the author's themes. The confusion of the scientists over the meaning, measurement, and accuracy of the I.Q. test is one such detail. It points out that the knowledgeable people Charlie wants to be like are very uncertain about their knowledge.
   a) What do these statements reveal about Charlie's understanding of the world at the beginning?
      (1) "I hope I have luck. I got my rabits foot and my lucky penny and my horse shoe." (page 625)
      (2) "I want to be smart like other people." (page 625)
      (3) "I had lots of tests and different kinds of races with Algernon. I hate that mouse. He always beats me." (page 626)
   b) Consider Fanny Girden's statement:
      "It was evil when Eve listened to the snake and ate from the tree of knowledge. It was evil when she saw that she was naked. If not for that none of us would ever have to grow old and sick, and die."
   How is this statement a metaphor for Charlie's desire for knowledge, his discovery of "naked" truths about his world, and his final deterioration?

7. What does Algernon represent to Charlie? What does he symbolize to the reader?

8. Why does Charlie leave to make a new beginning? Do you think he will be better off because of his past experiences, or will he again become the dupe of smarter people?

Interaction

1. What, if anything, is as important or more important to you than being accepted by others? How might Thoreau answer? How might James Baldwin? How might Charlie Gordon?
2. What admirable qualities does Charlie possess? Which of these qualities seem to you to be as important as intelligence? Does Charlie's society and ours value them as highly as intelligence? How does society's emphasis on intelligence, knowledge, and education affect you personally? In what way is Charlie's society anti-intellectual as well as excessive in its emphasis on intelligence?
3. One of the questions this story raises is, "To what extent does society have the right to tamper with the mind and personality of an individual?" Science and technology are experimenting today with methods of improving the human mind and body. What problems does such "improvement" raise?

On Individuality

Text pages 651–652

JAMES FENIMORE COOPER   1789–1851

All his life Fenimore Cooper was a pugnacious and outspoken individualist. Expelled from Yale (for insubordination), he turned to writing. He was moved by the failure of his first novel to persevere all the more and to quarrel publicly with his critics. By the mid-1800's he was a successful author of action adventures widely popular here and abroad, and was quarreling with his critics in court.

A professed foe of a society which encourages mediocrity instead of excellence, Cooper nevertheless sought to be imitative rather than original in his writing. He looked at literature as a way of expressing his convictions about America, not as an art. His careless, wordy, and affected style has continually disturbed readers, including the master of colloquial American prose, Mark Twain. In spite of the style, however, and in spite of Cooper's personal unpopularity, *The*

Last of the Mohicans, The Pathfinder, and *The Deerslayer* have been admired for their portrayals of frontier individualism. These *Leatherstocking* tales create Natty Bumppo, a hero of the wilderness who symbolizes a peculiarly American innocence and honesty.

Study Guide

1. What is the meaning of *mediocrity*? How does the "sway of numbers" result in mediocrity? Where do we see society's insistence on mediocrity in "Flowers for Algernon"?
2. Why is mediocrity dangerous according to Cooper?
3. Cooper seeks a balance between the individual and society. What limits on individual freedom does Cooper advocate?
4. What does Cooper mean by *individuality*?

Interaction

1. Neither Cooper nor Thoreau addresses himself to the material aspects of living in a democratic society. For example, neither one discusses the standard of living among underprivileged groups; nor do they express concern in their essays with making medical, educational, and other institutions more readily available to people in need of them. Rather they are interested in the *quality* of life in America. What do they consider basic to the good life?
2. Explain and illustrate your own definition of individuality. You may wish to start by agreeing or disagreeing with a statement or idea presented in this unit.
3. In what ways do the townspeople in "The Sculptor's Funeral" illustrate Cooper's ideas of mediocrity, "sway of numbers," and individuality? How do you think Cooper would have reacted to Emerson's "Self-Reliance"? (page 343)

Statement

Text pages 653–654

TECUMSEH   1768–1813

Tecumseh was born in the Shawnee village of Piqua near Springfield, Ohio, and as a youth took part in attacks on the white settlers. During the Indian wars and the conferences between the Indians and white men that continued for several years, Tecumseh displayed an eloquence and self-control that made him the foremost spokesman for the Indians. In an effort to offset the white man's advance, he formed a confederation of the Indian tribes from Canada to Florida. The 1811 Battle of Tippecanoe destroyed the confederacy. In the War of 1812 Tecumseh became a brigadier general in the British Army. He was killed in battle in 1813.

Study Guide

1. Tecumseh defends the principle of "squatter's rights," that is, the principle that since the red man was the first to arrive on the land, his presence should exclude all others. Was this a valid argument in the case of the Indians? How could it be used to support injustice? Are there any cases in which society has the right to take land away from its owner or the person who occupies it?
2. What is the Indian view of property ownership expressed by Tecumseh? How is it in conflict with the white man's view?

Interaction

1. As a special project, find out what happened to the Shawnee tribe after Tecumseh's death. Under what conditions do the Shawnees live today?
2. The protest of a minority — even a minority of one — is an expression of individuality basic to American culture. Thoreau's individual protest put him in jail. Tecumseh's ended in failure. How would Cooper explain the benefits of individual protest to society at large? What, in your opinion, is the value or danger of such protest?

The Unknown Citizen

Text page 655

W. H. AUDEN (biography pages 84–85)

Study Guide

1. Who are the "we" of this poem? Why have they erected a marble monument to JS/07/M/378?

2. From what sources did the State get its information about the citizen? What kind of information do these sources *not* reveal?
3. What values does this State prize the most?
4. What irony do you find in the following statements?
    a) ". . . everything necessary to the Modern Man,
       A phonograph, a radio, a car, and a frigidaire."
    b) "And our teachers report that he never interfered with their education."
5. Is the statement in the last line true? Why or why not?
6. In satirizing one kind of State, Auden implies that another kind of State would be better. What values do you think he is upholding?

Interaction

1. If you have read Orwell's 1984 you will see at once that it has much in common with this poem. When the State begins to dehumanize the individual, whose fault is it? What can be done about it?
2. Notice the frequent use of "our" in the poem. Is there something wrong when the State and its officials begin to think of *our* teachers, *our* Social Psychology workers? In your opinion, should it be *their*, that is, the citizens'?
3. The Roman emperors used to keep the masses quiet by providing them with "bread and circuses." Is this all that man needs? What are the equivalents of bread and circuses in the State that Auden portrays?

A Lone Striker

Text pages 656–657

ROBERT FROST   (biography pages 86–87)

Comments

A poem begins with a lump in the throat; a home-sickness or a love-sickness. It is a reaching-out toward expression; an effort to find fulfilment. A complete poem is one where an emotion has found its thought and the thought has found the words. . . . My definition of poetry (if I were forced to give one) would be this: words that have become deeds.

— ROBERT FROST

. . . there is a case against Robert Frost as a social philosopher in verse and as a representative of the New England tradition. He is too much walled in by the past. Unlike the great Yankees of an earlier age, he is opposed to innovations in art, ethics, science, industry, or politics.

— MALCOLM COWLEY: The Case Against Mr. Frost

In his pastorals, Frost's dominant motive is to reassert the value of individual perception against the fragmenting of experience resulting from modern technology. They thus deal with one of the most fundamental concerns of twentieth-century thought.

— JOHN F. LYNEN: Frost as Modern Poet

Study Guide

1. What is the situation described in the first stanza?
2. In what ways does Frost's striker differ from the usual striker?
3. How do we know that the striker is not just an idle, lazy, and selfish daydreamer?
4. What does the striker feel has happened to the importance of the individual human being? Which lines express this feeling?

Interaction

1. In what ways does Frost's striker contrast with JS/07/M/378?
2. This is a protest poem, or at least it records one man's protest. We have come to think of protest literature as angry or bitter. How would you describe the tone of this poem? Does the Lone Striker want to destroy the factory or the system that supports it?
3. What attitudes toward nature does Frost seem to share with Thoreau and Emerson?

from Spoon River Anthology

Text pages 658–659

EDGAR LEE MASTERS   1869–1950

Edgar Masters grew up in Petersburg and Lewiston, Illinois, the
area he later made famous as Spoon River country. After a year of
college, Masters went to Chicago, where he worked as a reporter and
began contributing poems and stories to magazines. Editor William
Reedy gave Masters a copy of *Epigrams from the Greek Anthology*,
which included ancient epitaphs. They inspired his *Spoon River
Anthology*, which attempts to portray the life of a whole town —
good people and bad, failures and successes. In each poem a former
resident of the town, now resting in the Spoon River graveyard, comments on the meaning of his own life.

Study Guide

1. Debate the following two interpretations of Oaks Tutt:
   a) Oaks Tutt was out of place in a town like Spoon River.
      The narrow-minded cynicism of townspeople like Jonathan
      Swift Somers stifled Oaks's idealism. The reference to Pon-
      tius Pilate's cynical question shows that Spoon River did
      not appreciate Oaks Tutt's spiritual insight and idealism.
   b) Oaks Tutt was a daydreaming, impractical idealist. Al-
      though he dreamed of the "wrongs of the world," he spent
      his time visiting cemeteries and ruins instead of real peo-
      ple. He did nothing to right the wrongs, let alone actually
      observe them. Somers exposed him for what he was.
2. Richard Bone was the stonecutter who carved the epitaphs for
   Spoon River's tombstones. Is he a hypocrite for engraving for
   posterity what he feels is false?
3. Richard Bone says that sometimes historians are influenced to
   hide the truth. Who might want the truth hidden and why?
   What specific examples can you think of in which history has
   been distorted?
4. What is Mrs. George Reece's formula for overcoming difficulty?
   Is it convincing?

Interaction

1. Write a letter of advice to Oaks Tutt from the point of view of one of the following:
   a) Thoreau
   b) Charlie Gordon
   c) Mrs. George Reece
   d) The State (as characterized in "The Unknown Citizen")
2. With your classmates, create a fictitious town or city. Select a name, location, and size. Then write a poem or a paragraph in the voice of one of the former townspeople buried in the local cemetery.

The Individual and Society: Summing Up

1. When writers take up the theme of the individual and society, they usually portray a conflict between the two. Generally speaking, if there is no conflict there is nothing to write about. Therefore it might be said that literature gives a distorted view of the relation between the individual and society because it ignores the millions of cases in which there is no conflict.

   On the other hand, it might be said that there is always some degree of conflict between the individual and society, even though it may be stronger in some cases than in others.

   In this unit the writers, speaking sometimes in their own voices, sometimes through their characters, give instances of individualism in action. Do you think any of these acts of individualism were excessive or unjustified?
2. Suppose someone said to Frost's Lone Striker: "What if everyone else did the same thing?" What reply would the striker make? What reply would you make?
3. With your classmates debate the following statements:
   a) The individual is always the best judge of what is good for him.
   b) Society cannot always be just to each individual because it must act, and when it acts it cannot take each individual equally into account.

OUR TOWN

Text pages 663–719

THORNTON WILDER *born:* 1897

Thornton Wilder is a writer with a philosophical bent, a writer who returns again and again to the questions of design and meaning in the universe. In *Our Town* he deals with birth, love, and death — the most universal things in man's existence. In *The Bridge of San Luis Rey* he searches for a sign of God's will in the collapse of a bridge. In *The Long Christmas Dinner,* a one-act play, and *The Skin of Our Teeth,* a play about man through the ages, he celebrates the cyclical pattern of life. "There is only one history," Wilder believes. "It began with the creation of man and will come to an end when the last human consciousness is extinguished." Wilder's best work expresses this philosophy of pattern and continuity in life.

Wilder was born in Madison, Wisconsin. His parents were interested in language and developed in their son a devotion to literature. When Wilder was nine, his father was appointed by President Theodore Roosevelt to be Consul General in Hong Kong. When the family returned to the United States, the Wilders settled in California. Wilder describes himself during these formative years as "a sort of sleepwalker. I was not a dreamer, but a muser and a self-amuser."

After attending Oberlin College, Yale, and the American Academy in Rome, Wilder taught French for four years. He then returned to school and wrote two novels while studying for his M.A. degree. The first novel, *The Cabala,* though not popular, was a critical success. But the second, *The Bridge of San Luis Rey,* startled Wilder's family and friends and Wilder himself by becoming an international best seller and prize-winning novel.

Since that beginning in 1927, Wilder has been a cultural ambassador and teacher as well as a leading experimental writer. For fifty years Wilder lived and worked in Connecticut. He then moved to Arizona, where he wrote *The Eighth Day.* Like *Our Town, The Eighth Day* is set in a small town at the turn of the century. In 1963 Wilder was awarded the Presidential Medal of Freedom and in 1965 the National Medal for Literature.

Wilder's interest in the theater developed over many years. He began by writing short plays for puppet theaters and by studying the Oriental drama. He was also an actor in several little-theater productions of his plays, and he has played the Stage Manager in several productions of *Our Town*. His experiments as a playwright are reflected in the works of both American and European dramatists. The German playwrights Dürrenmatt and Brecht acknowledged a debt to Wilder, and today's dramatists in America often dispense with the trappings of realism, just as Wilder did in *Our Town*.

Comments

In its brilliant current revival [1969], Thornton Wilder's *Our Town* seems to me better than ever. . . . As the era it depicts recedes into the distant past, its tribute to the ordinary people of the small New Hampshire community of Grover's Corners at the beginning of the century increases in importance as a celebration of America's lost innocence. . . .

— RICHARD WATTS, JR.: *The New York Post*

Through all misguided productions, *Our Town* survives in memory as an expression, mundane but still touching, of sublime optimism. Life, no matter how dull, is life.

— MEL GUSSOW: *The New York Times*

Study Guide

ACT 1

1. Howie Newsome's horse becomes "all mixed up about the route" in the opening scene. Why? What does this comment tell us about life in Grover's Corners?
2. Wilder wrote of *Our Town*, "I have set the village against the largest dimensions of time and place." How do the following devices in Act 1 suggest the "largest dimensions of time and place"?
   a) repeated use of the words *hundreds, thousands,* and *millions*
   b) historical and geological background
   c) the address on Jane Crofut's letter from her minister
   d) the discussion of the time capsule
3. What similarities do you see between the Gibbs and Webb families? How has Wilder underscored these similarities by his staging technique?

4. In what ways does the Stage Manager keep reminding us that this is a play and not real life? In what respects is the Stage Manager *omniscient* (that is, all-knowing)? Do you feel surprised when he says, "Doc Gibbs died in 1930"?

5. Besides the presence of the Stage Manager, what other devices remind the audience that they are in a theater, that the play is not reality itself, but a representation of reality?

ACT 2

1. The second act takes place many years after the first. How is the opening of Act 2 like the opening of Act 1? What do you think was Wilder's reason for making the openings similar?

2. What is Emily like as a high school student? (pages 694–698) What is George like? The Stage Manager says, "People are never able to say right out what they think of . . . marriage. You've got to catch it between the lines; you've got to *over*hear it." (pages 698–699) What seems to be George and Emily's attitude toward marriage? How does it compare with their parents' attitude? How does it compare with the attitudes of high school students today?

3. Wilder has his characters voice their misgivings before the wedding: Dr. and Mrs. Gibbs (pages 699–701) and George and Emily (pages 703–704). What attitudes toward marriage does Wilder reveal when he shows the "confusion way down in people's minds"?

4. How does the staging of the wedding (page 701) lead the audience to identify with the characters emotionally and at the same time to observe them objectively?

5. Act 2 is called "Love and Marriage." What universal or typical aspects of love and marriage does Wilder try to bring out? Does he give a believable picture of love and marriage, or does he idealize them? Give reasons for your opinion.

ACT 3

1. The third act takes place nine years after George and Emily's wedding. What changes have taken place in Grover's Corners? Are these changes important or only "skin-deep"?

2. "Choose the least important day in your life. It will be important enough," Mrs. Gibbs advises Emily. Does this turn out to be true? What insight does Emily discover about the gift of life?

3. "I never realized before," Emily says after death, "how troubled and how . . . how in the dark live persons are. From morning till night that's all they are — troubled." (page 712) Do the events in Acts 1 and 2 bear out Emily's statement?

4. What was Simon Stimson like in life? What is he like after death? In what ways are Mrs. Gibbs and Emily the same after death as they were in life? How are they different? Is Simon any less troubled and "in the dark" than he was in life?

5. How does Emily feel about death when she takes her place among the Dead? How do the Dead feel about death? How do they feel about life?

6. According to the play, the dead experience some sort of spiritual growth. Looking again at the Stage Manager's remarks on pages 707–708, describe this experience in your own words.

7. How are the references to big numbers, stars, history, and geology in Act 1 related to the events in Act 3? How does Wilder present death as a part of the life cycle, a process like birth and marriage?

THE PLAY AS A WHOLE

1. There is a breakfast scene in each act. How does each breakfast scene suggest the theme of the act? Which breakfast scene has the most emotional impact? Why?

2. "Our Town," Thornton Wilder wrote, "is not offered as a picture of life in a New Hampshire village. . . . It is an attempt to find a value above all price for the smallest events of our daily life." Which scene in the play expresses the idea that " the smallest events of our daily life" have a "value above all price"? What small events does Wilder value? Why does he feel they are so important? What "smallest events of our daily life" do you feel Wilder has *not* included?

3. Wilder never lets us become too involved in the story of George and Emily. Although we sympathize with them, we see their story in perspective. How do each of the following keep the audience detached?
    a) the use of the Stage Manager
    b) the treatment of time
    c) the juxtaposition of realistic close-ups with long shots of generalization
    d) audience participation
    e) the absence of a conventional plot

4. We first hear the hymn "Blest Be the Tie That Binds" in Act 1, as George and Emily are having a homework date — 1901 style. (page 680) We hear it again at George and Emily's wedding (page 703) and for a third time at Emily's funeral. (page 710) There are many versions of the hymn, one of which is excerpted below:

> Before our Father's throne,
> We pour united prayers;
> Our fears, our hopes, our aims are one;
> Our comforts and our cares.

> We share our mutual woes,
> Our mutual burdens bear;
> And often for each other flows
> The sympathizing tear.

> When we at death must part,
> Not like the world's, our pain;
> But one in God and one in heart,
> We part to meet again.

Explain how "Blest Be the Tie That Binds" reflects life in Grover's Corners and the themes of *Our Town*.

5. Is the total effect of the play one of joy, sadness, or a mixture of the two? If you were asked to place this play in either the section called "Dark Voices in American Literature" or "Voices of Affirmation," which would you choose?

Interaction

1. Compare and contrast Willa Cather's picture of small-town life in "The Sculptor's Funeral" (page 606) with Thornton Wilder's in *Our Town*. Note especially the similarities between Simon Stimson and Jim Laird.

2. Before *Our Town* was produced, Thornton Wilder asked an important man in the theater to read it. Wilder was later told, "Of course, you have broken every law of playwriting. You've aroused no anticipation. You've prepared no suspense. You've resolved no tensions." Do you agree with each of these criticisms? Does Act 1 build any suspense or raise any questions that you are anxious to have answered in Acts 2 and 3? How do you explain the continued popularity of *Our Town* and its frequent revivals on professional and amateur stages?

3. What do you think the Stage Manager would say about the effect of today's technology on the basic pattern of life? Do you think *Our Town* paints too rosy a picture of life? Does it give suffering, uncertainty, and injustice enough emphasis?
4. Adopting a voice more or less like the Stage Manager's, write an essay in which you introduce an audience to your community.
5. Look at the following newspaper article recently written about a school production of *Our Town*; then discuss the ways in which *Our Town* seems to you to be relevant or irrelevant today.

City Children Find "Our Town" Alien

When Thornton Wilder's *Our Town* opened on Broadway on Feb. 4, 1938, it was acclaimed for the universality of its picture of human life. Yesterday *Our Town* was again played in New York, but this time its audience — and even its cast — found an irrelevant, if enjoyable, exercise in play-acting.

"This person I'm playing — she doesn't seem real," 13-year-old Doreen Colon said of her role as Emily Webb, the girl who grows up to marry the boy next door and dies in childbirth. "I guess I'll get married, like her, but the rest of it — it doesn't have much to do with me."

Doreen and 18 other junior high school students presented the play as part of their work at a six-week summer program at the Jefferson Park Junior High School at 240 East 109th Street. Most of the cast had performed in other plays during the regular school year, but this was their first attempt at serious drama.

"We were looking for something new," Mark Walters, the drama coach, said in explaining the choice of Mr. Wilder's Pulitzer Prize-winning play. "We wanted to give them something about life as it is, and we figured this would do it."

At first, Mr. Walters said, he had planned to change the play's locale from Grover's Corners, New Hampshire, to East Harlem. Then he changed his mind — "Why try to improve on Thornton Wilder?" he explained — and reasoned that his students would be able to relate to the play's simple pattern of life and love and death.

But to the 13-year-olds and 14-year-olds in the cast, and to the 350 other summer school students who filled the dark and humid Jefferson Park auditorium yesterday morning, the pattern was too simple to be believable.

"The only criminal they had in the whole place was the town drunk — here we have mass murders," Eric Richards, the 13-year-old who played the drunk, remarked. "They could go to the top of the hill and watch the moon or the fog; but here, you watch the smog, and you have to carry a knife."

Bernard Johnson, 14, who portrayed Emily's father in the play, put it this way: "In a small town it's more painful if someone dies, because everyone knows everyone else. Here someone can die and no one knows — someone is dying right now, and I don't care."

A Different Era, Too

But to Bernard, the difference between life in New York and life in Grover's Corners was more than the difference between a big city and a small town.

"Life was much, much simpler then, even in the city," he said, shrugging in the manner of a middle-aged man who has found himself unable to cope with the vagaries of modern life. "Those were the golden years — no war, no crime."

For six weeks the cast members had read and discussed and rehearsed the words of *Our Town*. Yesterday, shortly before curtain time, others echoed Bernard's wistful thoughts of life as it should be.

"I wouldn't mind living in the country, away from all this," a little girl in braids said plaintively. Eric, the "town drunk," stared at the black and white paper flowers decorating the wooden stage and remarked sadly, "New York has the tallest buildings in the world, but the streets and the alleys are not very nice."

Yet, once the auditorium was filled and the lights began to dim, the scene backstage was no different from that of a hundred other school plays.

"They're all out there, hungry for us to make a mistake," a boy whispered. "I can't help it," a young actress said, thrusting out a trembling hand for her friends to see. "I can't make it stop moving."

Out front, in rows of hard wooden chairs, hundreds of children giggled and whispered. Mr. Walters stood up and waved a hand; slowly, the children quieted.

"This is the story of small town life," he told them. "This is a story of human beings." He sat down and the play began.

But it was not until the middle of the first act, when Rebecca Gibbs and her mother began to argue, that the audience first responded to the play, laughing and clapping at the familiar sight of a child defying a parent.

The loudest reaction of the morning came during the marriage ceremony in the second act. One of the assembled wedding guests, a young girl dressed to look like a middle-aged woman, turned to the audience with the inevitable line, "I just love weddings." The children waiting out front began to cackle, a few yelled "Shut up." Within a moment the auditorium filled with cheers and shouts.

Emily, the bride, appeared. Again the audience responded with shouts and cheers. The same thing occurred when the bridegroom kissed the bride.

And when the newly married couple ran down the steps from the stage and up the aisle to the back of the auditorium, leaving a trail of rice behind them, the audience clapped with a gusto dreamed of only by the most successful Broadway producer.

By noon the show was over and the children in the audience were on their way out to the waiting buses.

James Fonder, 11, a pupil at Public School 101, asked a friend, "Did they really get married?"

Anthony Ferguson, 9, looked at James with disgust. "It's just a play," he said, "a play about a boy and a girl."　　　 — *The New York Times*

LIFE CYCLES

Marianne Moore began a poem called "Poetry" with the words *I, too, dislike it.* Later in her poem she writes that good poems are *imaginary gardens with real toads in them.* The reader, then, must be prepared to see both the *imaginary gardens* and the *real toads.* He should not look at a poem as an autobiographical document, nor as a social commentary. He should see each poem as a symbol of feeling, and at the same time, as a statement about something genuine.

One poet's advice to students of poetry is to start by erasing everything you have ever heard about poetry: "Throw all this away and read them aloud," said Theodore Roethke. "Believe me, you will have no trouble if you approach these poems as a child would, naively, with your whole being awake, your faculties loose and alert. (A large order, I daresay!)"

Emily Dickinson 1830–1886

The poet who composed more than eighteen hundred poems, only three of which were printed during her lifetime, was almost overshadowed by the mystery surrounding her. The legends grew into conflicting biographies and wild speculations; even the undisputed facts were puzzling; and Emily Dickinson continues to haunt the literary world as an unaccountable ghost, impish and tragic by turns, perverse and puritan. As a girl she was said to have had many beaux. Although she was not frivolous, she was gay and quick-witted; her earliest writings — a teasing valentine, a school composition, a few random notes — disclose an irrepressible love of banter. Her face was a contradiction, a contrast of blandness and severity. Without being pretty, she was striking. She had dark, bronze-color eyes, white skin, and hair that was nearly Titian in brilliance. Declining a request for a photograph, she portrayed herself modestly but memorably: "I have no picture, but am small, like the wren; my hair is bold, like the chestnut burr; and my eyes, like the sherry in the glass that the guest leaves. Would this do just as well?"

Such self-references are rare. The physical events of her career were similarly few and plain. Daughter of a country lawyer, Emily Dickinson was born in Amherst, Massachusetts, December 10, 1830. She lived and died in the house in which she was born and, except for a few short trips, never left it. She had a happy childhood with an older brother, William Austin, and a younger sister, Lavinia. Yet, after her mid-twenties, she isolated herself, wrote countless poems but refused to publish them, saw practically nothing of the outside world, and luxuriated in being anonymous. . . . Emily Dickinson had suffered two great losses before she had reached her mid-twenties. Her first "dear friend and teacher" was Benjamin Franklin Newton, an ardent reader of unusual literature and a thinker out of tune with his times. He was twenty-seven and Emily was barely eighteen when she came under his influence. Three years after meeting her, Newton married a woman twelve years older than himself; two years later he died of tuberculosis. "When I was a little girl," Emily wrote to Thomas Wentworth Higginson, an influential man of letters who had become interested in her work, "I had a friend who taught me Immortality; but, venturing too near, himself, he never returned. Soon after, my tutor died and for several years my lexicon was my only companion. Then I found one more, but he was not contented I be his scholar so he left the land." The double loss was concentrated in her poetry, explicitly stated several times, notably in the lines beginning "I never lost as much but twice" and in two quatrains as poignant as they are famous:

> My life closed twice before its close;
> It yet remains to see
> If Immortality unveil
> A third event to me
>
> So huge, so hopeless to conceive,
> As these that twice befell.
> Parting is all we know of heaven,
> And all we need of hell.

The second parting was the more crippling. About a year after Newton's death, Emily visited with her father in Washington. She was midway between twenty-three and twenty-four. In Philadelphia she heard a sermon delivered by the Reverend Charles Wadsworth, admired the preacher, met him, and fell in love with him. He was forty, married, pastor of the Arch Street Presbyterian Church. Devoted to his work, he was probably unaware of the emotion he had aroused in the heart of his listener. Emily returned to Amherst, unable to shake off the spell woven by the minister and, unconsciously, by the man. There were two or three subsequent meetings — chance visits rather than the clandestine trysts darkly suggested by the townspeople — and an intermittent correspondence. Emily's hopes for greater intimacy must have been faint; nevertheless, they persisted. She dramatized them in her poetry; the woman and the craftsman united to find an outlet for the secret dream, the cherished moment of recognition, the always deferred delight and final disappointment.

For twenty-five years Emily Dickinson had kept herself to herself. She had loved music, but declining to join with others in the music-room, remained seated outside in the hall. She had sent little verses along with jellies and flowers to neighbors and their children, but she never visited them. After Wadsworth's death she was more alone than ever: "I do not yet fathom that he has died, and hope I may not till he assist me in another world." Eight months later she suffered a nervous breakdown . . . and died May 15, 1886. . . .

She had always declined to consider a publisher, and posthumous publication presented an unusually difficult problem. Over a thousand pieces of verse were unearthed in various places; they had been scribbled on the backs of recipes, on brown paper bags from the grocer, inside envelopes, and across small scraps of paper. There were often different versions of a stanza, and many alternate words were jotted down with no indication of a final choice. Lavinia Dickinson turned to Mabel Loomis Todd, a neighbor who had known Emily during the latter part of her life, and to Thomas Wentworth Higginson, the editor who had been consulted by Emily and who had been fascinated (and somewhat shocked) by her extraordinary images and verbal daring. Their first edited volume, entitled *Poems of Emily Dickinson*, contained 115 verses and appeared in 1890. . . .

Emily Dickinson's characteristic is not a single quality but a contradiction of styles. It is, for one thing, a paradox of reticence and flamboyance. Emily Dickinson made no innovation in the physical form of her poems, yet she was an indubitable innovator. She used the simple four-line stanza — the strict measure of the New England hymn-tunes — to sound a new and independent note in American poetry, a note which many other poets have attempted to echo. She startled her contemporaries and fascinated her admirers two generations later with a condensed, almost conversational, idiom: a sharp poetic speech which was an unrecognized rebuke to the loose rhetoric of her times. Her odd, "suspended" rhymes and her wry assonances, like the purposeful suspensions and dissonances of modern music, were forerunners of the "slant rhymes" and "half-rhymes" characteristic of twentieth-century poetry. Her sudden shifts from rich to lean phrases, her rapid juxtaposition of the trivial and the tremendous suggested a new poetic vocabulary.

There is no way of analyzing her unique blend of whimsicality and wisdom, no way of measuring her deceptive simplicity and her startling depths. The mystery of Emily Dickinson is not the way she lived but the way she wrote, a mystery which enabled a New England recluse to charge the literature of her country with poems she never cared to publish. — Louis Untermeyer

Comments

The enemy to all those New Englanders was Nature, and Miss Dickinson saw into the character of this enemy more deeply than any of the others. The general symbol of Nature, for her, is Death. . . . — Allen Tate

No one can read these poems or any of the tens of others like them without perceiving that he is not so much reading as being spoken to. There is a curious energy in the words and a tone like no other most of us have ever heard. Indeed, it is the tone rather than the words that one remembers afterwards. Which is why one comes to a poem of Emily's one has never read before as to an old friend.

But what then is the tone? How does this unforgettable voice speak to us? For one thing, and most obviously, it is a wholly spontaneous tone. . . . Poem after poem — more than a hundred and fifty of them — begins with the word "I," the talker's word. She is already in the poem before she begins it, as a child is already in the adventure before he finds a word to speak of it. To put it in other terms, few poets . . . have written more *dramatically* than Emily Dickinson, more in the live locutions of dramatic speech, words born living on the tongue, written as though spoken.

— ARCHIBALD MACLEISH

Study Guide

"Within That Little Hive," *text page 723*
1. In line 2 Emily Dickinson uses the phrase "Hints of Honey." What strength does the word *hint* have? In other words, suppose she had written "Stores of Honey" instead. What richness would the poem lose?
2. Describe an experience of your own when a dream seemed more real than reality — or when reality seemed only a dream.

"The Bird Her Punctual Music Brings," *text page 724*
If Emily Dickinson had used ordinary punctuation, she would probably have put a question mark at the end of line 6.

1. The first four lines of the poem imply that the bird has a special purpose on this earth. What is it?
2. In what sense is the bird's music *punctual?*
3. What words show the poet's sense of excitement? One of the things poetry does is to give us a new way of looking at familiar things. What new and surprising things are said about *work* and *rest* in this poem?
4. When work is *not* "electric rest" for a person, is there something wrong with the person or with the work? Do you know anyone for whom work is "electric rest"? What kind of work do you do which you do not think of as work?

"The Hummingbird," *text page 724*
Emily Dickinson did not usually give titles to her poems. Notice that all of her poems printed in the anthology, except this one, are titled after their first lines. So "The Hummingbird" is a title given

to the poem by her editors based upon evidence from an earlier draft of the poem that Emily did indeed have a hummingbird in mind. If you have observed one of these colorful birds you will know that it can almost stand still in mid-air on a blur of wings, and then dart to a new location with great speed.

1. Some definitions that might be helpful in reading the first stanza are: (a) *route:* a road taken or a specific course over which mail is sent; (b) *evanescence:* a vanishing away.

   What picture do lines 1 and 2 create?

2. The first 4 lines consist of exclamations and phrases rather than complete sentences. Suppose Emily Dickinson had written the following grammatically correct stanza:

   > The Hummingbird is
   > A Route of Evanescence
   > With a revolving Wheel.
   > The Hummingbird is
   > A Resonance of Emerald,
   > A Rush of Cochineal.

   In what ways do these "grammatically correct" lines change the poem? Do you feel that they spoil the poem? improve it? Why?

3. What natural action and reaction is captured in the words, "And every Blossom on the Bush/Adjusts its tumbled Head"?

4. Where is Tunis? Why does it seem to be just "an easy Morning's Ride" for the hummingbird? In what tone of voice would you read the last two lines?

5. Emily Dickinson once said, "All we secure of beauty is its evanescence." How does "The Hummingbird" illustrate this concept of beauty?

"Apparently With No Surprise," *text page 724*

1. How does Emily Dickinson's attitude toward nature in this poem contrast with her attitude in "The Hummingbird"?

2. What does this poem say about acceptance and resignation? about injustice? What else does it suggest to you?

"The Soul Selects Her Own Society," *text page 725*

   In this poem the word *majority* is used in a way that is no longer current; it means *greatness* or *superiority.* Lines 3 and 4 might be paraphrased like this: No more applicants for the Soul's Society need present themselves.

1. To what is the Soul compared? How does the whole poem carry out this metaphor?

2. Consider "The Soul Selects" as a poem about love. Readers who think that poems about love must "gush" should be surprised at Emily Dickinson's view of it. What words convey the idea that love has a harsh, uncompromising aspect?

3. Valves ordinarily are thought of as mechanisms used to stop the flow of air or water. Another connotation of the word which makes sense is the valves of the heart. The chariots pausing at the gate, the emperors kneeling at "her" feet all to no avail, suggest a heart (or Soul) closed to all other suitors.

If you looked up the word *valve* in an unabridged dictionary, you would find that the first meaning given there (although now archaic) comes from the Latin *valva*, meaning half of a double or folding door. Hence the references in the poem to doors and gates closing are picked up in the final stanza.

As you consider these possibilities, what, in your opinion, does the poem say about human relations? Do the rules of fair play mean anything to the Soul?

4. What effect does the word *stone* have, placed as it is in the poem?

5. Notice that the poem has only one perfect rhyme: *door-more.* All the others are off-rhymes, like *Society-Majority.* What other off-rhymes can you find?

"After Great Pain," *text page 725*

The poem — through its images of stiffness, numbness, stone, lead, and freezing — re-creates the aftermath of pain and shock.

In the anthology the poem is printed exactly as it was found in Emily Dickinson's manuscripts. However, it seems fairly clear that she reversed the order of two lines in the second stanza as she copied the poem. The stanza seems to make better sense this way (and here we have used ordinary punctuation):

> The feet, mechanical, go round
> a wooden way;
> Of ground, or air, or ought
> regardless grown —
> A quartz contentment like a stone.

1. What kind of pain — physical or psychological — does the poem deal with?

2. What words and phrases in the poem suggest lifelessness?

3. Usually we think of *contentment* as meaning "satisfaction" or "happiness," but what kind of contentment is this (line 9) if it is "like a stone"?

4. In the last stanza Emily Dickinson makes a comparison between two experiences. One is the subject of the poem — the "Hour of Lead" which comes "after great pain." The second experience is that of a freezing person lost in the snow. What is the point of the comparison? That is, how are the two experiences alike?

"Because I Could Not Stop for Death," *text page 726*

1. Personification is one of the most common devices in poetry, and Emily Dickinson uses it frequently. We have seen personification in most of her poems in the anthology: the blossom in "The Hummingbird"; the flower, the frost, and the sun in "Apparently With No Surprise"; the soul in "The Soul Selects Her Own Society"; the nerves, the heart, and the feet in "After Great Pain."
   What is personified in "Because I Could Not Stop for Death"?
2. How do the images in stanza 3 symbolize stages in the human journey?
3. Discuss the following statements about the poem:
   a) The journey described in the poem is like the final journey to the cemetery.
   b) The journey is like a wedding journey — a bridegroom bringing his bride home.

Interaction

1. For years Emily Dickinson's poems were known only in versions edited by friends and relatives. These editors "corrected" her unique way of punctuating and capitalizing words. They also sometimes changed the wording of a poem when they found it too "odd." In 1955 an edition of Emily Dickinson's poems was published, following her original manuscripts and using all her dashes and capital letters. This is the edition we have followed in IDEAS AND PATTERNS.
   Here are two stanzas in "regular" style. Compare them with the originals on page 725:

> I've known her from an ample nation
> Choose one;
> Then close the valves of her attention
> Like stone.

> This is the hour of lead,
> Remembered if outlived,
> As freezing persons recollect the snow —
> First chill, then stupor, then the letting go.

After comparing the versions, consider whether the regularized version gains in clarity over the original. Which version is more expressive? Why?

2. In 1891 Andrew Lang wrote, ". . . if poetry is to exist at all, it really must have form and grammar, and must rhyme when it professes to rhyme." Lang went on to say that Emily Dickinson is not really a poet because her rhymes are imperfect, her grammar not always perfectly correct. What imperfect rhymes did you notice in the poems? What "incorrect" usage and grammar? Do you agree that Emily Dickinson is a poor poet because her rhyme and grammar are often irregular? Explain.

Susan Miles, a British critic, wrote that Emily's half-rhymes and nonrhymes were intended to "defeat the reader's expectation." Miss Miles writes that the nature poems tend to be regular, musical, and harmonious, especially when they celebrate the harmony in nature. But in poems about human discord and the disharmony in the universe, the rhymes are irregular. Do the poems you have read support this explanation? Explain by giving examples from the poems.

The World's Turning

The Snow Man

Text page 727

WALLACE STEVENS 1879–1955

Wallace Stevens lived most of his life in Hartford, Connecticut, where he was vice-president of a large insurance company. People often found it hard to accept the fact that one of America's greatest poets was also an important business executive. Stevens himself, however, thought it was a good thing for a poet to "share the common life." Most of Stevens's neighbors and associates knew him only as a rather prosperous businessman. When a friend wrote him to say that he had met someone from Hartford who had never heard of Wallace Stevens, the poet replied:

It did not surprise me to find myself unknown in the Navy or even to a man from Hartford. I try to draw a definite line between poetry and business and I am sure that most people here in Hartford know nothing about the poetry and I am equally sure that I don't want them to know because once they know they don't seem to get over it. I mean that once they know they never think of you as anything but a poet and, after all, one is inevitably much more complicated than that.

In another letter Stevens wrote: "It is odd that people should think business and poetry incompatible and yet accept business and almost anything else as all in a day's work."

And so he often walked to work in the morning, jotting down his poems on pieces of paper as he walked. When he got to the office he gave his notes to his secretary to type up.

Study Guide

1. What the poem says, more or less, is that only a snowman could avoid certain thoughts and emotions as he looks at a wintry landscape. According to the poem, what feelings does winter stimulate in sensitive observers?

2. Many poets dislike talking about their poems; they want the poems to speak for themselves. Wallace Stevens, however, often received letters from readers asking him to explain his work, and he never hesitated to answer their questions. He said of this poem: "I shall explain 'The Snow Man' as an example of the necessity of identifying oneself with reality in order to understand it and enjoy it."

   As you read the poem does it give you a sense of winter? Does it make the reader identify with wintry sights and wintry thoughts?

dandelions

Text pages 728–729

Deborah Austin *born:* 1920

Miss Austin teaches at Pennsylvania State University and is the author of *The Paradise of the World*, a book of poems.

Study Guide

1. In this poem Deborah Austin compares the dandelions to troops in battle. What picture of the dandelions does she draw in the lines on the following page?

a) "the troops took over" (line 2)
b) "the barrage continued/deafening sight" (lines 12–13)
c) "pow by lionface firefur pow by
   goldburst shellshock pow by. . . ." (lines 20–21)

2. Why are the words *pow, whoosh,* and *splat* appropriate and effective? What other "sound effects" did you notice in the poem?

3. The "battle" takes place over two days — yesterday and today. But "tomorrow smoke drifts up." The dandelions are now "wrecked battalions" and "smoke/drifts/thistle-blown/over the war zone. . . ." What change has taken place in the dandelions?

4. What are the "guerrilla snipers"? The poet says that they will "never/pow/surrender." What does the reader know will eventually happen to them?

5. In what way is nature like war according to this poem?

After Apple-Picking

Text pages 730–731

ROBERT FROST   (biography pages 86–87)

Study Guide

1. On one level this poem is about just what it says it is about — the thoughts of a man who is tired and drowsy after a whole day spent picking apples. On another level this poem is about human seasons, about life. Considering this larger meaning of the poem, then, what do the following lines tell us about the speaker's past — the "harvest time" of his life?

> There were ten thousand fruit to touch
> Cherish in hand, lift down, and not let fall.

2. In line 7 Frost writes, "Essence of winter sleep is on the night," and throughout the poem winter is associated with sleep. At the end of the poem the woodchuck's sleep (hibernation) is contrasted with "This sleep of mine, whatever sleep it is." (line 38) What essential contrast between men and animals do you suppose Frost seeks to imply here?

3. The speaker says, "One can see what will trouble/This sleep of mine. . . ." (lines 37–38) Do you think he has regrets about his life? That is, has he done everything he wanted to do or could have done? Support your answer with quotations from the poem.

from Snowbound

Text pages 732–733

JOHN GREENLEAF WHITTIER 1807–1892

Unlike the other New England poets (Bryant, Holmes, Longfellow, and Lowell), John Greenleaf Whittier was a poor man. He earned just enough to support himself and his mother and sister by writing, editing a newspaper, and serving in the Massachusetts legislature. As a public man, he was one of the first to speak against slavery. He was at times attacked by angry, egg-throwing crowds and saw his newspaper office burned by a mob. Although Whittier's first commitment was to abolition, he also worked for the betterment of women, American Indians, and the blind.

Whittier was born on a Haverhill, Massachusetts, farm to a Quaker family. When the Civil War began, he retired to his home state to write *Snowbound*. This long nature poem, a departure from his political poems, brought him a comfortable income for the rest of his life.

Study Guide

1. What distinction does the poet want his reader to make between *portent* and *threat*? (line 7)
2. What visual image does Whittier create in lines 11 through 13?
3. **Syntax.** What is the direct object of the verb *told*? (line 14) That is, what did the "coming of the snowstorm" tell or warn them about?
4. Compare the imagery of lines 1 through 18 with that of the remaining lines. What is the main difference?

Auspex

Text page 733

JAMES RUSSELL LOWELL 1819–1891

Although the New England poets are often thought of as stodgy men of letters, James Russell Lowell, one of the leading New England poets, was known for his exuberance and liveliness. As a student at Harvard he would occasionally leap over columns in the Harvard Yard and crow like a rooster. In later life, as a critic of Thoreau, Whitman, and himself, he was tough and biting.

Lowell was one of the Boston Lowells, a leading New England family. His father was a minister and he himself intended to be a lawyer. But the law held little interest for him, and he soon became involved in abolition and other social movements. For a time he wrote editorials for the *Pennsylvania Freeman*, an antislavery periodical, and concentrated on political writing. In 1848 he published *A Fable for Critics*, a light satire on noted literary figures of the day (including Whittier, Hawthorne, and James Fenimore Cooper). *Fable* included some now famous couplets: Of Edgar Allan Poe, Lowell wrote,

> There comes Poe, with his raven, like Barnaby Rudge,
> Three fifths of him genius and two fifths fudge.

Study Guide

1. **Plain sense.** Because poetic language is often more compressed than ordinary conversation, it is sometimes helpful to take the time to examine the "sentences" in a poem. In line 1 to what does *it* refer? To what noun does *Nest* in line 2 refer? *Days* in line 4 is the simple subject of a sentence. What is its simple predicate? What does *they* in line 7 refer to?
2. Lowell wrote this poem at a time when he realized that he was fast growing old. How does his description of the season and the birds show us his thoughts about oncoming age?
3. What do you think the poet means when he says, "My heart . . . had songbirds in it"? How will the dreary days affect him as a man? as a poet?
4. After looking at the footnote for the word *auspex* on page 733 of the anthology, comment on the significance of the title.

The World's Turning: Interaction

1. Why do you think that poets so often find symbolic significance in the seasons?
2. Make a list of the things you associate with each of the four seasons. If you like, put your associations in the form of a poem.

Love

If You Should Go

Text page 734

COUNTEE CULLEN 1903–1946

Born in Baltimore and orphaned at an early age, Countee Cullen was adopted by the Reverend Frederick Cullen and raised in New York City. Cullen attended New York University where he won scholastic honors and prizes for his poetry. While still an undergraduate he wrote his first published volume of verse, *Color,* and while attending graduate school at Harvard, Cullen composed his next two collections, *The Ballad of the Brown Girl* and *Copper Sun.* After living in France on a fellowship, Cullen returned to New York to teach French at Frederick Douglass High School, where he taught for eleven years before his early death. Cullen's works include a novel, *One Way to Heaven,* and many poems, the best of which Cullen himself selected for *On These I Stand.* "If You Should Go" shows one side of Countee Cullen — the romantic lyric poet greatly influenced by Edna St. Vincent Millay. Cullen was also the poet of Harlem and its people. He wrote of their "joys and sorrows — mostly," he said, "of the latter."

Study Guide

1. In the first stanza, Cullen compares love to day and night. What phase of love is like day? What phase is like night?
2. In stanza two how does he compare love to a dream?
3. How is this poem an expression of the impermanence of love?

If I Should Learn

Text page 734

EDNA ST. VINCENT MILLAY 1892–1950

At the age of nineteen Edna St. Vincent Millay became famous with her poem "Renascence." After graduation from Vassar College in 1917, Miss Millay moved to New York where she associated with many of the leading young artists and writers and saw the publication of her first book *Renascence and Other Poems*. Among her publications in the early twenties was *A Few Figs from Thistles*, a collection of verse that seemed to speak for the young people of the Jazz Age; they responded to the poet's vitality, unconventionality, and romanticism. But these and later poems have come to be regarded as more than expressions of youthful rebellion. They reveal Miss Millay's mastery of the sonnet, her command of simple lyric and ballad forms, and her gift for deep psychological penetration.

After her marriage Miss Millay settled in New England and continued to write. Although her work ranges from a libretto for an American opera to journalism attacking European dictators, she is read today as one of the finest poets of America.

Study Guide

1. How does the speaker feel about the man she is talking to in this poem?
2. How would she feel if she heard that he had died? How would she behave? Why would she behave this way?
3. Edna St. Vincent Millay was one of the most accomplished sonneteers America has produced. Notice that the poem is a single sentence. The first 8 lines are an introductory subordinate (or dependent) clause. The last 6 lines form the main (or independent) clause. What change of tone do you see in the last 6 lines?

The River-Merchant's Wife: A Letter

Text page 735

EZRA POUND   1885–1969 ·

Ezra Pound was born in Hailey, Idaho, but lived most of his life in Europe, where he was involved with most of the new movements in art and literature in the first half of this century. He was a friend and supporter of such writers as T. S. Eliot, Robert Frost, William Butler Yeats, James Joyce, Ernest Hemingway, and William Carlos Williams.

Pound began as an advocate of art for art's sake, but as the years went on he became more and more interested in economics and politics. It seemed to him that art could not flourish in a sick society. Like so many American writers, such as Emerson and Thoreau, he set out to preach to his fellow citizens. Pound saw civilization as a struggle between men (such as Dante, Jefferson, and Confucius) who fought for clarity, honesty, and a decent society, and those (mostly financiers and militarists) who ran the world in the interests of their own greed and power. His long epic poem *Cantos* is about this struggle. The last published line of the *Cantos* puts his ethic concisely: *To be men not destroyers.*

The final, tragic years of Pound's life came from his involvement with Italian Fascism during the Second World War. Living in Italy at the beginning of the war, Pound made the mistake of broadcasting over the Italian radio. He saw himself as a prophet who was warning Americans of the dangers they faced in their own society; the American government saw him as a traitor. When the American troops swept into Italy after the war he was arrested and placed in a detention camp near Pisa. There he wrote the *Pisan Cantos,* in which he described himself as "a lone ant from the broken anthill of Europe."

Pound was never brought to trial for treason. He was judged insane and placed in a mental hospital in Washington. After many years he was released and allowed to return to Europe. In his old age his ferocity left him and he lapsed into long silences, torn by doubts about the value of his own work:

> That I lost my center
> > fighting the world.
> The dreams clash
> > and are shattered.

"The River-Merchant's Wife" is from *Cathay,* an early book of translations from the Chinese. Pound did not know Chinese; he worked from the notes of an American scholar. In spite of his many errors in translation, Pound was intuitively closer to the spirit of Chinese poetry than most translators who had a knowledge of the language. T. S. Eliot called Pound "the inventor of Chinese poetry for our time."

Study Guide

1. **Syntax.** Each language has its own grammatical structures, and that of Chinese is very different from that of English. Pound's

art in this translation has allowed him to combine good, clear English with a suggestion of the way the Chinese language works. For example, in a Chinese poem each line forms a completely separate unit. In "The River-Merchant's Wife" you will notice that most of the lines express complete thoughts: for example, the line *Called to, a thousand times, I never looked back.* In Chinese, this line would consist of five Chinese characters (each word is its own character) which might be literally translated

thousand   call   not   one   turn (-head)

Where else in the poem do you find lines or phrases which do not quite sound like "English" but rather suggest a "Chinese" way of expressing things?

2. In this poem Pound has also tried to capture the manners and customs of another culture. In the Orient people behave more formally with each other than Americans do. Even close friends and members of a family observe a more structured relationship. What kind of letter would a young American girl write to an absent husband or boyfriend? Is the love expressed by the Chinese girl less intense because of her formality?

3. What change took place in the young bride between the ages of fourteen and fifteen?

Interaction

1. Throughout this book we have looked often at the ways in which nature is used in poetry, often to reflect a human season or human feelings. Oriental poetry uses nature symbolism perhaps even more than does Western poetry. In this poem, what is suggested by the following?
    a) "the river of swirling eddies," (line 16)
    b) "The monkeys make sorrowful noise . . ." (line 18)
    c) "the moss is grown . . . Too deep to clear them away!" (lines 20–21)
    d) "The leaves fall early this autumn . . ." (line 22)
    e) "The paired butterflies are already yellow with August" (line 23). What is suggested by the fact that the butterflies are *paired*?
2. Compare Pound's poetic translation with the literal translation by Wai-lim Yip on the following page:

The Song of Ch'ang-kan

My hair barely covered my forehead.
I played in front of the gate, plucking flowers,
You came riding on a bamboo-horse
And around the bed we played with green plums.
We were then living in Ch'ang-kan.
Two small people, no hate nor suspicion.
At fourteen, I became your wife.
I seldom laughed, being bashful.
I lowered my head toward the dark wall.
Called to, a thousand times, I never looked back.
At fifteen, I began to perk up.
We wished to stay together like dust and ash.
If you have the faith of Wei-sheng.[1]
Why do I have to climb up the waiting tower?
At sixteen, you went on a long journey
By the Yen-yü rocks at Ch'ü-t'ang
The unpassable rapids in the fifth month
When monkeys cried against the sky.
Before the door your footprints
Are all moss-grown
Moss too deep to sweep away.
Falling leaves: autumn winds are early.

---

[1] Wei-sheng had a date with a girl at a pillar under the bridge. The girl did not show up. The water came. He died holding tight to the pillar. (From *Shih Chi.*)

   The waiting tower in the next line, literally, is wait-for-husband tower or rock which alludes to a story of a woman waiting for the return of her husband on a hill. One version has it that she was turned into a rock while waiting.

Where Have You Gone . . . ?

Text page 736

MARI EVANS

Mari Evans is a musician as well as a poet. She lives in Indianapolis, Indiana, and edits a magazine for an industrial firm. Her poems are often light and whimsical.

Study Guide

1. This poem has a "talky" quality that you can hear best if you read it aloud. Where would you come to a full stop before beginning each new "sentence"? What tone of voice do you think should

be used in reading this poem — serious, ironic, or a mixture of the two?

2. Some of the ideas and expressions in this poem resemble closely the ideas and expressions in many love songs and love poems. What commonplace ideas and expressions do you find here? Do you think they are clichés?

3. What does "the rent money in one pocket" tell about the character of the man the speaker loves? What new meaning does it give to the phrase, "your crooked smile" (lines 4 and 19)?

4. How is the situation of this poem different from the situation in "The River-Merchant's Wife"?

Love: Interaction

1. How does Edna Millay's reaction to pain in "If I Should Learn" (page 734) compare with Emily Dickinson's in "After Great Pain"? (page 725)

2. Shakespeare wrote, "Men have died from time to time, and worms have eaten 'em, but not for love." How do each of the poets in this section differ in their treatment of love? Would the following writers be likely to agree or disagree with Shakespeare that men don't die for love: Thornton Wilder, Emily Dickinson, Edna St. Vincent Millay, Mari Evans?

3. Bring to class a poem in which the poet treats love in a lightly humorous or ironic way. You may wish to write your own poem or look at the poems of writers such as Dorothy Parker, John Donne, or William Shakespeare. An excellent source is *The Book of Humorous Verse* in almost all libraries.

Loss and Decline

Elegy for Jane

Text page 737

THEODORE ROETHKE   1908–1963

Theodore Roethke has been called one of the best poets America has produced. He has also been called childish, competitive, self-destructive, and tragic. The facts of his life are simple enough: He was born in Saginaw, Michigan; educated at the University of Michigan and Harvard; and he taught at several colleges and universities. In 1954, *The Waking*, a book of poems, won the Pulitzer Prize.

But these simple facts hardly touch Roethke as a man, as a poet, and as a teacher. Like Poe, Roethke was besieged with fits of depression. The fear of encroaching madness tortured him, and in his darkest moods he jotted these lines into his journal:

- I rasp like a sick dog; I can't find my life.
- An intense terrifying man: eating himself up with rage.
- It's all I can do, he said, to hold on to life.

Yet Roethke considered himself a hopeful man. Much of his poetry, although it doesn't ring with Whitmanesque affirmation, does express a guarded optimism. "In spite of all the muck and welter," he wrote, "the dark, the *dreck* [garbage] of these poems, I count myself among the happier poets."

As a teacher Roethke was devoted and creative; but he often wished that grading papers and student problems took up less of his time and energy, which he would have liked to devote to his poetry. "Elegy for Jane" is a poem written on the occasion of the death of one of his students.

Study Guide

1. In the speaker's mind, Jane and her ways are like things in nature. For example, he compares her curls to "tendrils" and calls her "My sparrow." Find other comparisons between Jane and nature. Which one suggests her delicacy? her shyness? her moods?
2. How does the speaker try to console himself? Is he successful?
3. Roethke writes that he speaks words of love for Jane, even though he has "no rights in this matter." What are the qualities in Jane and her world that he mourns for?

Ex-Basketball Player

Text page 738

JOHN UPDIKE   *born:* 1932

John Updike made his reputation as a writer while still in his early twenties. Born in Shillington, Pennsylvania, he was educated at Harvard, where he edited the humor magazine, *The Lampoon*.

After studying in England, Updike went to work on *The New Yorker*, the home of two writers he admired and imitated — Thurber and Benchley. He then left the magazine to concentrate on his own writing, and produced an astonishing number and variety of novels, short stories, light verse, sports reports, book reviews, parodies, obituaries, and profiles. In his fiction and poetry Updike likes to look at the deeper significance of the commonplace. "Everything can be as interesting as every other thing," he says. "An old milk carton is worth a rose."

Study Guide

1. In your own words, describe the contrast between Flick's high school days and his present situation.
2. **Symbol.** Look at the description of Pearl Avenue in lines 1–4. In what way is Pearl Avenue just like Flick's life?
3. One of the ways in which Updike brings home the contrast between Flick's past and present is by drawing some comparisons. For example, he writes, "His hands were like wild birds" in stanza 2; in stanza 3 he writes, "His hands are fine and nervous on the lug wrench." How do the gas pumps described in stanza 1 remind us of a basketball team?
4. Updike tells us that Flick jokes about the old days: "Once in a while,/As a gag, he dribbles an inner tube." But the last three lines show Flick sitting at the lunch counter, staring off into space and nodding "towards bright applauding tiers. . . ." What is Flick daydreaming about? What do the rows of candy remind him of?
5. As we read this poem, we become aware of the speaker's feelings as well as Flick's. What are the speaker's feelings toward the change that has taken place in Flick's life?
6. In your estimation what went wrong with Flick's life?

Gert Swasey

Text pages 739–741

Winfield Townley Scott 1910–1968

For most of his life, Winfield Townley Scott kept close to his New England home, editing the Providence, Rhode Island, *Journal* and writing about the New England scene. He spent the last years of his life in the Southwest as literary editor of the *New Mexican*. He always described himself as a "literary fellow," dividing his time between editing and writing poems. Yet there is nothing "literary" about Scott's poetry — "literary," that is, in its worst sense. ". . . I have had at least one consistency," he said, "and that is the use of a basically simple vocabulary. Chalk it up to non-intellectuality if you want to. I know dazzling effects can be got with the strong and the esoteric, but they are not my kind of thing."

Study Guide

1. The first lines of the poem give us a capsule history of Gert Swasey. This is not an unusual way of beginning a poem. Epic poets begin their poems with the "argument," the basic outline of the poem. What does Scott's opening do to capture our interest?
2. Gert did many vastly different things during her lifetime. What was she like? How did the town feel about her?
3. Why does the poet want the "ladies" to hear about, to think about Gert Swasey? Whom does he seem to admire more — Gert or the ladies he is addressing?

Blue Girls

Text page 742

JOHN CROWE RANSOM   *born:* 1888

John Crowe Ransom's poetry is almost at the opposite end of the emotional scale from Walt Whitman's expansive and optimistic verse. Ransom's poems are soft-spoken, controlled commentaries on the frail human estate. Often he gives us dramatic snatches of a tragic life, but he plays down the sentiment. His main characters are losers, though not without honor, and he gently mocks them. With the irony characteristic of his poetry, Ransom once assured people that he does indeed feel emotion: "Assuredly I have a grief and am shaken — but not like a leaf."

A native of Pulaski, Tennessee, Ransom identified himself with a group of young Southern writers opposed to industrialism and technology. In the magazine *The Fugitive*, which Ransom helped found, and in *I'll Take My Stand*, a collection of essays by Ransom and eleven other Southerners, these writers urged a return to an agrarian way of life, a refined and eminently civilized way of life they associated with the Old South. Many of Ransom's best poems — "Here Lies a Lady" and "Parting, Without a Sequel," to name two — are set in this atmosphere of the aristocratic Old South.

Study Guide

1. The girls in this poem are "blue" because they are wearing blue school uniforms. As the speaker watches them what feelings does he have? Does the sight bring him joy? sorrow? or a mixture?
2. In the final stanza Ransom contrasts the blue girls with "a lady with a terrible tongue." What lesson to the blue girls is implied in this contrast?
3. Shakespeare and other poets used a convention in which they often stated that their love, or the beauty of their beloved, would never die because it would be preserved forever in their poems. How does Ransom in the third stanza turn this convention inside out? What does he suggest about the power of poetry to "preserve" beauty?

Hurt Hawks

Text pages 742–743

ROBINSON JEFFERS 1887–1962

Robinson Jeffers's pessimism places him among the "dark voices" in American poetry. Born in Pittsburgh, Pennsylvania, Jeffers studied medicine and forestry before deciding that he was interested only in poetry. The death of a rich relative left him independently wealthy. He and his wife settled in Carmel, California, where he built an impressive stone house with his own hands. In this house he lived out the rest of his life, writing poetry about the sharp and ironic contrast between the magnificence of nature and the baseness of mankind. (See line 18 in "Hurt Hawks": "I'd sooner, except the penalties, kill a man than a hawk.") In one of his most misanthropic moods, Jeffers wrote, "Cut humanity out of my being; that is the wound that festers."

Study Guide

1. In Part I Jeffers describes how the hurt hawk looked when he found him, and he imagines how it must have felt. It is not, however, the physical pain that Jeffers is deeply concerned about. He is more concerned with the things that happen to the hawk as a result of its wound. What are some of these things? (See lines 6–10.)

2. Lines 12–17 tell why "no one but death the redeemer will humble that head." These lines also tell us why Jeffers's sympathy and admiration for the hawk are so great. What are some of the noble qualities that Jeffers describes in these lines?

3. Part II of the poem tells us about the poet's part in the hawk's story. What had the speaker tried to do for the hawk? Did these efforts succeed? Which lines tell you the answer?

4. In what respect is the hawk's death noble and heroic?

5. You may find the last two lines troublesome. They speak of something which "Soared" after the hawk was shot, and we immediately wonder what *it* could be. Suggest as many possibilities as you can. There is no need to arrive at a single answer.

Loss and Decline: Interaction

1. Compare the town in which Gert Swasey lived with Grover's Corners, the town in Thornton Wilder's play.

2. Two of the poems in this group — "Elegy for Jane" and "Hurt Hawks" — are about death. What is different about each poet's sense of loss and treatment of death?

3. Which of the poems in this group say something about waste — wasted opportunity, a wasted life? In your opinion, was Gert Swasey's life a waste? Why or why not?

Life Cycles: Summing Up

1. Emily Dickinson once wrote: "Parting is all we know of Heaven/ And all we need of Hell." How do the following react to parting from a loved one?
    a) Countee Cullen, "If You Should Go" (page 734)
    b) Edna St. Vincent Millay, "If I Should Learn" (page 734)
    c) the wife in "The River-Merchant's Wife" (page 735)
    d) Mari Evans, "Where Have You Gone . . . ?" (page 736)
    e) Theodore Roethke, "Elegy for Jane" (page 737)

2. Select one of the poems in this section for an especially close reading. Practice reading it aloud with expression and clarity. Look at the poem analytically for a moment. What do you notice about the rhymes, the rhythm, sound effects, images, metaphors, similes, and tone? What experience or emotion do you think the poet tried to express? Is this poem as effective in reaching the reader's emotions as other poems in this section? Why or why not?

3. Ezra Pound defined great literature as "language charged with meaning to the utmost possible degree." Which lines from the poems in this section best fit this description?

4. Robert Frost wrote that "Poetry provides the one permissible way of saying one thing and meaning another." He was referring, of course, to the poet's use of figurative language. What figures of speech or comparisons do you notice in "After Great Pain," "The Snow Man," "dandelions," "After Apple-Picking," "Auspex," "Elegy for Jane," and "Ex-Basketball Player"? Does only poetry make these figures of speech "permissible," or would they also be appropriate in an essay? a conversation? a speech?

EXPERIMENT IN THE TWENTIETH CENTURY

Gertrude Stein

Text pages 747–749

GERTRUDE STEIN   1874–1946

Gertrude Stein was a member of a wealthy American family. After studying psychology at Radcliffe and medicine at Johns Hopkins, she moved to Paris, where she remained for most of her life, making only one return visit to the United States. In Paris she began collecting paintings by artists who were little known and little understood, among them Matisse and Picasso. By the end of her life she had put together one of the world's greatest collections of modern art.

Since she had an independent income, Miss Stein could afford to be as "noncommercial" and "experimental" as she wished. Although during her lifetime the audience for her own books was small, she had an enormous influence on other writers. When occasionally she had a popular success, as she did with *The Autobiography of Alice B. Toklas,* she was delighted. Most of her writing is very hard to follow, however, because she used such things as character, plot, and description in ways we are not accustomed to.

One of Gertrude Stein's most enjoyable pieces is the text of the opera *Four Saints in Three Acts,* for which Virgil Thompson wrote the music. An RCA Victor recording is available.

Study Guide

1. Look at the passage from *The Making of Americans* on pages 748–749 of the anthology. In spite of the fact that the punctuation, capitalization, and grammar often violate the rules we learn in school, do you find the writing clear? Or is it hard to follow? Are there any points at which normal punctuation would have made this paragraph easier to read?
2. Which of the three poems from *Tender Buttons* (page 748) do you think is most successful in suggesting the subject named in its title? Why?

from U.S.A.

Text pages 750–756

JOHN DOS PASSOS   *born:* 1896

John Dos Passos, born in Chicago, has lived in many parts of the U.S., Mexico, and Europe. During World War I he was active in the ambulance and medical services and drew on his experiences for his first successful novel, *Three Soldiers*, which, like *The Red Badge of Courage*, explodes the myths about war. In 1937 Dos Passos published *The 42nd Parallel*, 1919, and *The Big Money* under the title *U.S.A.* This trilogy is Dos Passos' major contribution to American literature.

Dos Passos writes in a way that most of us aren't used to; clearly, he doesn't follow the conventions of capitalization and punctuation. More important, he doesn't build step by step to a logical conclusion. For example, in "The Camera Eye" sections he skips around, using free association or *stream of consciousness*. Writers use this when they want to capture the flow of the mind in all its shifts, interruptions, and illogic. The "Newsreel" is another example. It is "kaleidoscopic"; it fits pieces of reality — newspaper clippings, advertisements, songs — together to create a mood.

Dos Passos intersperses the narrative of *U.S.A.* with many brief "Newsreel" and "The Camera Eye" sections. The selections included in the anthology are "The Camera Eye (29)" and "Newsreel XLV."

Comment

Dos Passos is actually one of the few American writers of his generation who has been inspired by the industrial landscape and has sought to duplicate some of its forms in *U.S.A.* He has taken from technology the rhythms, images, and above all the headlong energy that would express the complexity of the human environment in the twentieth century. . . .

What Dos Passos wants to capture more than anything else is the echo of what people were actually saying, exactly in the style in which anyone might have said it. The artistic aim of his book, one may say, is to represent the litany, the tone, the issue of the time in the voice of the time, the banality, the cliché that finally brings home to us the voice in the crowd — the voice of mass opinion.

— ALFRED KAZIN: John Dos Passos — Inventor in Isolation

Study Guide

1. **The Camera Eye.** This excerpt from *U.S.A.* takes us into the mind of a young soldier in World War I. What has the soldier been doing that day? What will he be doing in the near future? What do you think is the main thing on his mind? What is the hammering he hears?

2. **Newsreel.** Dos Passos went to many sources for his "Newsreels." Find examples here of popular songs, commercials, and news stories. The advertisement for an automobile is probably a word-for-word transcription of a real advertisement. What comment on American society is Dos Passos making by including this ad?

3. **The Campers at Kitty Hawk.** The biography begins and ends with the famous first flight. What shifts in time sequence did you find in this biography? What different points of view does Dos Passos use in this piece? We do not get a personal glimpse of the Wright brothers here. Instead, Dos Passos shows us how Wilbur and Orville were part of their times, products of their times:

   "the Wright brothers got backers,
      engaged in lawsuits,
      lay in their beds at night sleepless with the whine of phantom millions. . . ."

   How does the story of the Wright brothers, as Dos Passos sees it, fit in with the theme of materialism in the "Newsreel"? Look at the biography of the "young man on the way up," paragraph 2 of the "Newsreel." How do Wilbur and Orville fit that rags-to-riches pattern?

4. **Style.** What does Dos Passos use instead of capitalization and punctuation to help us read with the right pauses and tones? Did you find that his style made reading difficult? What do you think are the advantages and disadvantages of using the "kaleidoscopic" style, stream of consciousness, shifts in time sequence, shifts in point of view, and different kinds of print?

5. **Allusion.** In "The Campers at Kitty Hawk" Dos Passos alludes to the fifteenth-century painter and scientist Leonardo da Vinci. What did Leonardo have in common with Wilbur and Orville Wright?

6. **Diction.** "The Camera Eye" has been described as a "poetic reverie." Dos Passos uses unusual and vivid word combinations to create dreamlike states. His phrase "the winey thought of death" is one example of his poetic use of language. Find other examples.

Interaction

Compose a "Newsreel" for today. Use snatches of songs, head-lines, broadcasts, commercials, political speeches, fashionable slang, and so forth. Try to gear your choices to create *one* distinct impression of the present moment in the U.S.A.

The Jilting of Granny Weatherall

Text pages 757–766

KATHERINE ANNE PORTER   *born:* 1890

Katherine Anne Porter began writing as a child in Texas, where she was born. As a young woman she traveled in Europe and Mexico and worked as a reporter and editor in New York. Her first successful collection of stories was *Flowering Judas*. Her best-known works are *Pale Horse, Pale Rider*, a collection of three short novels, and *Ship of Fools*, a novel.

Study Guide

1. What is Granny's attitude toward Doctor Harry? Father Connolly? her children? Has her well-organized, busy existence helped her to live with her emotional problems? Explain your answer.
2. Do you feel that these quotations are an accurate representation of the way a very old lady's mind might work?
   a) "She had spent so much time preparing for death there was no need for bringing it up again. Let it take care of itself now." (page 759)
   b) "So . . . this is my death. . . . Oh, my dear Lord, do wait a minute. I meant to do something about the Forty Acres. . . . I meant to finish the altar cloth and send six bottles of wine to Sister Borgia. . . ." (pages 765–766)
3. **Structure.** Granny's stream of consciousness flows gradually from the present to the long past. Letters from John and George are mentioned on page 759. At what point does the reader realize who John is? At what point is George identified?
4. Who is Hapsy? She is not mentioned in Granny's review of her children on page 762; she isn't physically present at the bedside at the story's end. Relate your answer to the following passage:

It was Hapsy she really wanted. She had to go a long way back through a great many rooms to find Hapsy standing with a baby on her arm. She seemed to herself to be Hapsy also, and the baby on Hapsy's arm was Hapsy and himself and herself, all at once. . . . Then Hapsy melted from within and turned flimsy as gray gauze and the baby was a gauzy shadow. (page 763)

5. Do you find Granny's last name symbolically significant? What does the name Hapsy suggest?
6. Granny's recollection of her jilting is hellish. She tries to repress it. Is there any love for George left in her? If so, how does she deal with it?
7. What was the great disappointment of Granny's life? What is it that — at the moment of death — she cannot forgive? (page 766)

Interaction

1. Miss Porter treats death in this story in terms of images of court-ship and love. Compare her strategy with that of Emily Dickinson in "Because I Could Not Stop for Death." (page 726)
2. "After Apple-Picking" by Robert Frost (page 730) permits several levels of interpretation. According to one of these, the poem is the musings of a man approaching death. After re-reading "After Apple-Picking," do you find this interpretation a valid one? Why or why not? To what extent are Granny Weatherall's concerns and dreams similar to those of the apple-picker?

Shoes

Text pages 767–769

JOHN WIDEMAN

Mr. Wideman is a young writer who teaches at the University of Pennsylvania.

Study Guide

1. Like "The Jilting of Granny Weatherall," "Shoes" uses the stream of consciousness technique to go back and forth in time. It is also a story about death. How did Eugene die?
2. The "she" in the story (first mentioned in the third paragraph)

is probably Eugene's mother and the narrator's grandmother. What are the stages in her acceptance of Eugene's death? How do you explain the "morning walks to the gate"?

3. How does the narrator cope with the fact of Eugene's death, in contrast to Eugene's mother? In your own words, describe the importance of the shoes to the narrator.

4. As a boy the narrator cried one night when the family started talking about Eugene. What are some of the things that made him cry? (page 769) The author ends his story with, "but the tears stopped and the forks and knives rang louder and the leaves drifted silently like sand to fill the holes he had made." (page 769) The images suggest the passing of time. What effect does time have on the narrator's adjustment to Eugene's death?

Interaction

1. In the section "Life Cycles," you read poems in which a season or something else in nature became a symbol for a man's mood "The Snow Man," "After Apple-Picking," "Auspex"). What is the importance of the "high piles of leaves" in "Shoes"? That is, what season is it and how does the season suit the mood of the narrator?

2. Literature of many ages and countries has themes and forms in common. This is true of the theme of death, which has concerned writers since time immemorial — for obvious reasons. Like "Shoes," many of the selections in your text deal with death. Think, for a moment, about these selections:
    a) "Texas Massacre" (page 65)
    b) "On a Naked Hill in Wyoming" (page 66)
    c) The three poems on the Civil War (pages 261–263)
    d) Jim's death in *The Red Badge of Courage* (pages 421–425)
    e) *Spoon River Anthology* (pages 658–659)
    f) Act 3 of *Our Town* (page 705)
    g) "Because I Could Not Stop for Death" (page 726)
    h) "Elegy for Jane" (page 737)
    i) "Hurt Hawks" (page 742)
    j) "The Jilting of Granny Weatherall" (page 757)
What are some of the different treatments of the theme? Which ones do you feel are the most effective?

3. Write one or two paragraphs in which you experiment with the stream of consciousness technique. You may wish to relate a personal experience or describe a place.

General William Booth Enters into Heaven

Text pages 770–772

VACHEL LINDSAY   (biography page 25)

General William Booth was a revivalist preacher in England, known for his fundamentalist religious teachings and his compassion for society's outcasts. In 1865 he founded the Salvation Army, which set up missions to help outcasts; two years later Salvation Army missions were extended to the United States. In later life General Booth lost his sight (see line 24) but continued his work. In this poem Lindsay pictures Booth's ascension into heaven after his death in 1912. The ascent is likened to the revival meetings Booth held as leader of the Salvation Army.

Comment

In one way Lindsay was traditional — he did not follow the dominant tendency toward free verse, already announced by the Imagists and soon to be accelerated by the influence of Sandburg, Masters, and many lesser poets. Lindsay's innovations in form occurred within a traditional and primitive convention, that of the folk ballad. However, he heightened its rhythmic character and its violence.

— BRADLEY, BEATTY, LONG: The American Tradition in Literature

Study Guide

1. Who follows General Booth on his journey to Heaven? Why are "unwashed legions" more appropriate here than "clean-cut" or pious followers? What happens to Booth's followers when they reach Heaven?
2. Lindsay tells us in the subtitle that "Are you washed in the blood of the Lamb?" is taken from a hymn. What effect does Lindsay achieve by repeating this line in each stanza?
3. Lindsay selects many different instruments for each section of the poem. How are the drums, flutes, banjos, and so forth appropriate to the sections they accompany? Why does Lindsay call for "no instruments" at the end?
4. What picture does Lindsay give us of Booth as a man?

5. This poem has been set to music by Charles Ives and is available through any record store and many libraries. Quote lines and phrases from the poem in which the sounds (or sound effects) support the meaning.

Interaction

What does this poem have in common with spirituals, such as "When the Saints Go Marchin' In" or "Didn't It Rain?" (page 180) How does "General William Booth Enters into Heaven" differ in form and tone from Lindsay's "The Flower-Fed Buffaloes"? (page 104)

In a Station of the Metro

Text page 773

EZRA POUND   (biography pages 172–173)

The "metro" of the title refers to the Paris subway system. The two lines of this tiny poem are connected by a semicolon instead of the words *is like*.

Study Guide

1. What do the petals correspond to? What does the black bough correspond to?
2. How is this poem like a haiku? What is the advantage of keeping the poem short?

Interaction

The Imagist movement in poetry did not last long: most of the poets who proclaimed themselves Imagists found that their own theories were too restrictive. Thus Ezra Pound abandoned strict Imagism when he began writing his *Cantos*; the presentation of pure images did not allow him room to include his own commentaries on politics, economics, and other matters.

Although there are few pure Imagist poems read or written today, the movement was an important one. The Imagists thought that poetry had become too soft, too filled up with sloppy adjectives, too mindlessly pretty. They wanted to cut back to the hard essence of poetry, and so they decided to do away with direct comment and with "emoting." They would present a sharp image and let the image itself convey the emotion to the reader. Thus "In a Station of the Metro" says nothing about how Pound felt when he saw the crowd in the subway. The image of the crowd is swiftly presented with a vivid metaphor: that is all.

Pound's friend William Carlos Williams was strongly influenced by Imagism. See his poem "Young Woman at a Window" on page 776 of the anthology. A picture is presented: whatever comment or emotion the reader finds in it is implied, not stated. Williams's "The Red Wheelbarrow," also on page 776, would be a strict Imagist poem except for the comment in the words "so much depends."

As an exercise, write one or two short Imagist poems. Make your reader *see* something with a few well chosen words. Eliminate all personal comment about your own ideas or emotions. Make your adjectives few and sharp.

William Carlos Williams 1883–1963

As the short biography on page 774 says, William Carlos Williams was both a doctor and a poet. "Both seem necessary to me," he wrote. "One gets me out among the neighbors. The other permits me to express what I've been turning over in my mind as I go along."

The reader never feels Williams went searching for subjects for poems. Objects and events merely "happen" in a Williams poem, the way they would to anyone who is feeling alive and just going about the business of living. There are five poems by Williams in the anthology. Notice how each of them captures a moment close up, as if on film.

Comment

The first thing one notices about Williams's poetry is how radically sensational and perceptual it is: "Say it! No ideas/but in things." Williams shares with Marianne Moore and Wallace Stevens a feeling that almost nothing is more important, more of a true delight, than the way things look. . . .

— RANDALL JARRELL: *Introduction to* William Carlos Williams: Selected Poems

Study Guide

"The Act," *text page 774*

1. What is the difference in the attitudes of the man and the woman in the poem? How do their attitudes toward the roses show their different attitudes toward life?
2. Why is the poem called "The Act"? What is the main "act" or action in the poem?
3. Notice how Williams has stripped his poem to the very essentials of the moment. He doesn't tell us, for example, who the people are, what they were doing before the poem begins, where they are, what the setting (a garden?) looks like. Would any of this information enrich the poem? Another poet could have made from this encounter a poem three times as long. What is the value of keeping a poem as short as possible?

"The Artist," *text page 775*

1. The first half of the poem describes Mr. T.'s execution of a ballet step. Why does Williams call his poem about Mr. T. "The Artist"? Who is Mr. T.? That is, do you think he is really a dancer?
2. The second half of the poem describes the impact of Mr. T.'s dance on his audience. Why was the mother "taken by surprise" and left "speechless"? How does the fact that the mother is confined to an "invalid's chair" add to the drama?
3. Between them, the artist and his audience created something ideal, something perfect. What did each contribute?
4. The poem ends with Mr. T.'s wife coming in from the kitchen. She has missed the scene — "the show was over." Do you think that the scene could have been repeated for her benefit with the same electric effect?
5. What does the poem imply is the relationship between Mr. T. and his wife?

"Young Woman at a Window," *text page 776*

1. Unlike "The Act" and "The Artist," "Young Woman at a Window" is not a dramatic scene. Rather, it is a picture — a still life photograph. Where does the speaker seem to be standing?
2. Williams does not tell us why the young woman is crying. What universal story (or stories) does the picture suggest? What other pictures of a mother and child does this picture recall?
3. This poem is actually a single sentence. The subject and verb

("She sits") are followed by a series of prepositional phrases. Look for a moment at the following rearrangements of the poem:

   a) She sits with tears on her cheek, her cheek on her hand, the child in her lap, his nose pressed to the glass.

   b) She sits with tears on her cheek,
      Her cheek on her hand,
      The child in her lap,
      His nose pressed to the glass.

Do you find either of these arrangements as satisfactory as Williams's? Why or why not?

"This Is Just to Say," *text page 776*

1. As in "The Act" there are two people in this poem, but we are told very little about them. Who do you think they are?

2. Which line contains the most vivid sense impression? How does the rest of the poem make this line stand out sharply?

3. Compare the eating of the plums with the cutting of the roses in "The Act."

"The Red Wheelbarrow," *text page 776*

The wheelbarrow, the chickens, the rain in this poem are no more than that. They are not symbols, and there is no story behind them. There is only one question to ask about this poem: Why does "so much depend" upon these objects?

William Carlos Williams: Interaction

1. Williams wrote in his poem "A Sort of a Song": "No Ideas/but in things." What unusual "things" does Williams select to write about? Do his poems contain "ideas" as well? Explain.

2. Walt Whitman's poem "There Was a Child Went Forth" opens with these lines:

   There was a child went forth every day,
   And the first object he look'd upon, that object he became,
   And that object became part of him for the day or a certain part
      of the day,
   Or for many years or stretching cycles of years.

Consider "The Red Wheelbarrow" for a moment as a childhood recollection which moves the speaker. Describe a similar "snapshot" from your own childhood — a brief, visual image that remains in your mind.

E. E. Cummings 1894-1962

Edward Estlin Cummings, born in Cambridge, Massachusetts, received his education at Harvard University. Before America entered World War I, Cummings served as an ambulance driver in France. He was later imprisoned on an unfounded charge of treason, and he recorded his experience in *The Enormous Room*. After serving in the United States Army as a private, Cummings studied art in Paris. He was a professional painter as well as a poet for the rest of his life.

In 1923 Cummings published his first volume of poetry, *Tulips and Chimneys*. The many tender lyrics and biting satires which followed are in his *Collected Poems*. Cummings is noted for his romantic attitude toward rebellion, his reverence for children, and his joyous and playful moods. He often printed his name as *e. e. cummings*, another playful symbol for his revolt against a conforming and mechanized society.

Comment

The poems to come are for you and me and not for mostpeople. — it's no use trying to pretend that mostpeople and ourselves are alike. Mostpeople have less in common with ourselves than the squarerootofminusone. You and i are human beings; mostpeople are snobs.   — E. E. CUMMINGS

Study Guide

"nobody loses all the time," *text pages 777-778*
1. The reader sees Uncle Sol through the eyes of his nephew. The poem, then, characterizes the speaker as well as Uncle Sol. What is the nephew's definition of success? Account for his attitudes toward vaudeville and farming. Where does his word choice reveal his set of values?
2. What seemed to be Uncle Sol's philosophy of life? By what standards might he be seen as successful? Do you regard him as a tragic figure? Explain.

"in Just–," *text page* 779

1. What indicates that the poem is spoken by a child or by an adult who is using the language of children? Try reading the poem aloud, using appropriate expression. How does Cummings provide "stage directions" for reading the poem?

2. The poem contains a lot of parallel and repeated phrases, for example: "when the world is mud-/luscious" (lines 2–3) and "when the world is puddle-wonderful." (line 10) Find other parallel and repeated phrases.

3. **Allusion.** An allusion to the god Pan is made in "the goat-footed/balloonMan." The footnote on page 779 explains that Pan was a god of revelry. He is usually shown playing his flutelike pipe and leading the shepherds in dance across the fields. He has the legs of a goat and is a god of spring, joy, and celebration. How is the balloonman like Pan? Why is it appropriate to allude to Pan?

4. This poem is about a very special time of year and its effect on children, who seem to be able to sense it and express its mood. What precisely is the season? What is the weather like? What is the mood?

"anyone lived in a pretty how town," *text pages* 780–781

In this poem verbs are used as nouns, impersonal pronouns as proper names. The main character is "anyone." The woman who loves him is "noone." Cummings may have named her "noone" because she is "just a nobody," an ordinary person. The "someones" and "everyones" appear to be the town's leading citizens, the type of people that would consider "anyone" and "noone" unimportant.

1. How do the "Women and men (both little and small)" treat "anyone"?

2. What do the children of the town guess? What change takes place in the children when they grow up?

3. What sort of person is "noone"? How do she and "anyone" differ from the rest of the town? In the fifth stanza Cummings describes the lives of the "someones" and "everyones." What sort of lives do they lead?

4. How are "noone" and "anyone" buried? Which line suggests that they become part of nature after death?

5. Why does Cummings use names like "anyone," "noone," "everyone," and "someone" instead of specific names?

6. **Unconventional grammar.** As a rule, what part of speech is *how*? What is its function in line 1? Move the *how* in the sentence

until you find a slot in which it makes more sense. Replace some of Cummings's odd selections of words with more conventional words. What does the poem lose with the more conventional wording?

7. A repeated refrain in the poem is "Sun moon stars rain." There are also references to the turning seasons. How is this use of the seasons, the planets, and the weather like that in *Our Town?*

"i thank You God," *text page 781*

1. What argument against doubt does the poem present? Is it based on "reason" or on "feeling"?
2. In the last two lines Cummings is talking about people who are deaf and blind, but not through physical afflictions. What does it mean to have the ears of your ears asleep and the eyes of your eyes closed? Give some specific examples.
3. What does Cummings mean by "the sun's birthday"?

E. E. Cummings: Interaction

1. How is the experience in "i thank You God" like Emily's experience in the third act of *Our Town?*
2. Compare this poem with the following selections, all of which are about man's relationship to God:
   a) "Go Down, Moses" (page 180)
   b) "Didn't It Rain?" (page 180)
   c) "The Maypole of Merry Mount" (page 187)
   d) "Meditation Six" (page 228)
   e) "The Creation" (page 229)
   f) "A True Sight of Sin" (page 267)
   g) *From* "Sinners in the Hands of an Angry God" (page 269)
   h) "To a Waterfowl" (page 353)
   i) "The Chambered Nautilus" (page 354)
   j) "General William Booth Enters into Heaven" (page 770)
   If you have not read all of these selections, limit your discussion to those you have read. Write a short paper on "Different Attitudes of Man Toward God," drawing upon the literature for specific examples.

Experiment in the Twentieth Century: Summing Up

1. Perhaps none of the writers included in this section would have called their work "experimental." They may simply have thought

that they had found the right way to express their ideas. But let us assume that these new techniques were "experiments." Now the word *experiment* implies breaking new ground, attempting something different from the traditional forms. Which of the following "experiments" do you think successful, which failures? Perhaps some of them appear to you as only partly successful. Give reasons for your answers:

    a) Gertrude Stein's "Celery" (page 748)

    b) John Dos Passos' compressed impressionistic biography of the Wright brothers in "The Campers at Kitty Hawk" (page 752)

    c) The stream of consciousness technique in "The Jilting of Granny Weatherall" (page 757) and "Shoes" (page 767)

    d) The musical accompaniment indicated by Vachel Lindsay for "General William Booth Enters into Heaven" (page 770)

    e) The way William Carlos Williams breaks the lines into phrases in "The Artist" (page 775)

    f) E. E. Cummings's use of spacing, small and capital letters, and run-together words in "in Just–" (page 779)

2. In what sense is every work of literature an experiment — even when its form is most traditional? See, for example, Edna St. Vincent Millay's "If I Should Learn." (page 734)

3. Many writers who were experimental in their time have become so accepted that their work no longer looks different in any way from traditional writing. For example, Stephen Crane's way of recording psychological processes in *The Red Badge of Courage* was new in Crane's day. Hemingway's spare writing has been so widely imitated that it no longer seems unusual.

    Of course every form was at one time new, "experimental," even the sonnet. Why do you think many writers want to use new techniques? Why aren't traditional forms always good enough?

Glossary

abhor (ab·hor′). To hate.

abject (ab′jekt). Disheartened.

aboriginal (ab′ə·rij′ə·nəl). Primitive.

abstruse (ab·stroos′). Difficult to understand.

acme (ak′mē). The highest point.

acoustics (ə·koos′tiks). Sound-producing qualities of a room or auditorium.

affront (ə·front′). Insult.

ague (a′gyoo). Chill.

altercation (ôl′tər·kā′shən). Angry argument.

amelioration (ə·mēl′yə·rā′shən). Improvement.

anathema (a·nath′ə·mə). A curse.

anomalous (ə·nom′ə·ləs). Irregular; abnormal.

antediluvian (an′ti·di·loo′vē·ən). Pertaining to the time before the Flood; primitive.

appellation (ap′ə·lā′shən). Name or title.

badlands. A barren area covered with peaks, ridges, and mesas cut by erosion.

bard. A poet.

bellicose (bel′ə·kôs). Warlike.

beseeching. Begging; imploring.

blatant (blā′tənt). Loud and noisy.

brevet (brev′it). A promotion awarded for achievement on the field of battle.

canny (kan′ē). Cautiously shrewd.

catapultian (kat′ə·pult′ē·ən). Like an engine for hurling stones or arrows.

cipher (sī′fər). A person of no value or importance.

clamber (klam′bər or klam′ər). To climb, using hands and feet.

cognizance (kog′nə·zəns). Knowledge; recognition.

commensurate (kə·men′sə·rit). Adequate; in proper proportion.

compunction (kəm·pungk′shən). Twinge of conscience.

conciliate (kən·sil′ē·āt). To overcome the hostility of.

congruity (kən·groo′ə·tē). Agreement; fitness.

conjecture (kən·jek′chər). Guess.

contemplative (kən·tem′plə·tiv or kon′təm·plā′tiv). Thoughtful.

contrivance (kən·trī′vəns). Machine.

coquetry (kō′kə·trē). Flirtation.

corpulent (kôr′pyə·lənt). Fat.

cowled (kould). Hooded.

cretin (krē′tin). A person showing mental dullness (colloquial).

debauch (di·bôch′). To deprave and corrupt.

debris (də·brē′). Remains of something destroyed; rubble.

decorous (dek′ər·əs). Proper.

deference (def′ər·əns). Courteous respect.

deities (dē′ə·tēz). Gods.

demotic (di·mot′ik). Popular.

deprecating (dep′rə·kāt′ing). Apologetic.

derisive (di·rī′siv). Mocking.

diffidently (dif′ə·dənt·lē). Shyly; timidly.

din. To repeat insistently.

disconcert (dis·kən·sûrt′). To confuse; perturb.

disconsolate (dis·kon′sə·lit). Gloomy; dejected.

dissonance (dis′ə·nəns). Discord.

dogged (dog′id). Stubborn.

edifice (ed′ə·fis). A building.

eloquent (el′ə·kwənt). Convincing; fluent.

ephemeral (i·fem′ə·rəl). Lasting but a short time.

equinox (ē′kwə·noks). Point or time at which the sun crosses the celestial equator, when the days and nights are equal in length.

equivocal (i·kwiv′ə·kəl). Having a doubtful meaning; ambiguous.

PRONUNCIATION KEY: add, āce, câre, pälm; end, ēven; it, īce; odd, ōpen, ôrder; took, pool; up, bûrn; ə = a in *above*, e in *sicken*, i in *flexible*, o in *melon*, u in *focus*; yoo = u in *fuse*; oil; pout; check; go; ring; thin; this; zh, vision.

ethereal (i·thir'ē·əl). Celestial.

ethical (eth'i·kəl). Moral.

exhortation (eg'zôr·tā'shən). Plea; warning.

exigency (ek'sə·jən·sē). Necessity.

expatriated (eks·pā'trē·āt'əd). Banished.

extant (eks'tənt). Still existing.

façade (fə·säd'). The front part of a building.

facetious (fə·sē'shəs). Given to flippant humor, especially at an inappropriate time.

feign (fān). Make a false show; pretend.

felicitate (fə·lis'ə·tāt). To congratulate.

festoon (fes·tōōn'). A chain of flowers and leaves.

formidable (fôr'mid·ə·bəl). Fearsome; inspiring dread.

fracas (frā'kəs). A noisy fight.

frivolous (friv'ə·ləs). Foolish.

fusil (fyōō'zəl). A flintlock musket.

galling (gô'ling). Very irritating.

gamin (gam'in). Homeless youngster.

gauntleted (gônt'lit·əd). Wearing gloves.

gesticulate (jes·tik'yə·lāt). Express by gestures.

girted (gurt'əd). Surrounded.

glibness (glib'nəs). Ability to speak fluently without much thought or sincerity.

gyrate (jī'rāt). Revolve.

hackneyed (hak'nēd). Commonplace; worn out by over-use.

harangue (hə·rang'). Deliver a lengthy, loud speech.

harassed (har'əsd *or* hə·rasd'). Tormented; pursued with annoyances.

huckster. Peddler.

ilk. Class or kind.

impetus (im'pə·təs). Energy or force.

imprecation (im'prə·kā'shən). Curse.

inaccessible (in'ak·ses'ə·bəl). Not capable of being reached or approached.

incarnation (in'kar·nā'shən). The assumption of human form; a person or thing in which some ideal is embodied.

indigenous (in·dij'ə·nəs). Native to a place or country.

indigent (in'də·jənt). Poor.

infamy (in'fə·mē). Disgrace.

inordinate (in·or'də·nit). Excessive.

inscrutable (in·skrōō'tə·bəl). Difficult to understand; mysterious.

insipid (in·sip'id). Dull; lacking flavor or spirit.

insoluble (in·sol'yə·bəl). Incapable of being solved or explained.

interposition (in'tər·pə·zish'ən). Interruption; interference.

invincible (in·vin'sə·bəl). Unconquerable.

invulnerable (in·vul'nər·ə·bəl). Not capable of being injured; unconquerable.

jaded (jād'əd). Weary.

jocosity (jō·kos'ə·tē). Witticism.

jurisprudence (jōōr'is·prōōd'ns). Science or system of law.

laurel (lor'əl). A crown of laurel leaves, worn as a symbol of honor; distinction for outstanding achievement.

legerdemain (lej'ər·də·mān'). Sleight of hand; trickery.

loweringly (lou'ər·ing·lē). Frowningly; sullenly.

lucid (lōō'sid). Clear; easily understood.

ludicrous (lōō'də·krəs). Ridiculous.

lugubrious (lōō·gōō'brē·əs). Mournful.

lurid (lōō'rid). Shocking; also, lighted with a yellowish-red glare.

magnanimity (mag'nə·nim'ə·tē). Generosity.

malady (mal'ə·dē). Illness.

malediction (mal'ə·dik'shən). A curse.

maniacal (mə·nī'ə·kəl). Violently insane.

maudlin (môd'lin). Overly sentimental.

melee (mā'lā). A confused, hand-to-hand fight.

moniker (mon'ə·kər). Name or nickname (colloquial).

morbid (mor'bid). Showing excessive interest in gruesome and unwholesome matters.

motley (mot'lē). Many-colored.

mummery (mum'ər·ē). A performance by people in masks and disguises; a hypocritical ritual.

munificent (myōō·nif'ə·sənt). Generous.

natty (nat'ē). Neatly and smartly dressed.

notorious (nō·tor'ē·əs). Widely known and disapproved of.

nubbin (nub'in). Anything small and undeveloped.

nuptial (nup'shəl). Pertaining to marriage or a wedding.

obdurate (ob'dyə·rit). Stubborn.

obscurity (əb·skyŏŏr'ə·tē). Darkness; the quality of being unclear.

obsequious (əb·sē'kwē·əs). Overly submissive and obedient; servile.

obsolete (ob·sə·lēt'). Outdated.

ocelot (os'ə·lət). Tiger cat.

occult (ə·kult'). Secret; mysterious; having to do with magical arts.

ocular (ok'yə·lər). Relating to the eyes or sight.

ominous (om'ə·nəs). Threatening evil.

omnipotent (om·nip'ə·tənt). All-powerful.

paean (pē'ən). A song of joy or praise.

pallid (pal'id). Pale.

pandemonium (pan'də·mō'nē·əm). Riotous uproar.

paradoxical (par'ə·doks'ə·kəl). Seemingly contradictory.

pariah (pə·rī'ə). Outcast.

parody (par'ə·dē). A humorous imitation of a serious work.

paroxysm (par'ək·siz'əm). A sudden and violent outburst.

pathos (pā'thos). Quality that arouses pity.

peon (pē'ən). Servant.

perambulate (pə·ram'byə·lāt). Stroll; walk so as to inspect.

peremptory (pə·remp'tər·ē). Positive; intolerant of opposition.

pernicious (pər·nish'əs). Very harmful; deadly.

perspicacious (pur'spə·kā'shəs). Having keen understanding.

perturbation (pur·tər·bā'shən). Worry; disorder.

pestilential (pes'tə·len'shəl). Harmful; like a plague or disease; annoying.

petulant (pech'ŏŏ·lənt). Peevish; insolent.

pinion (pin'yən). A toothed wheel driving or driven by a larger wheel.

pinnacle (pin'ə·kəl). The highest point or place.

placid (plas'id). Calm.

plowshare (plou'shâr'). Blade of a plow.

poignant (poin'yənt). Painful to the emotions, such as *poignant* grief.

pomp. Splendor; magnificent display.

pompous (pom'pəs). With exaggerated self-importance.

portentous (pôr·ten'təs). Foreboding evil.

potent (pōt'nt). Powerful.

precious (presh'əs). Affectedly delicate or sensitive.

precipitous (pri·sip'ə·təs). Very steep; hasty.

prescience (prē'shē·əns). Foresight.

presumptuous (pri·zump'chŏŏ·əs). Arrogant; unduly bold.

prodigious (prə·dij'əs). Enormous.

prostrate (pros'trāt). Lying with face on ground.

proverbial (prə·vûr'bĭ·əl). Spoken like a proverb; well known.

prowess (prou'is). Strength and skill.

proximity (prok·sim'ə·tē). Nearness.

pyre (pīr). A heap of materials arranged for burning a body at a funeral.

ragamuffin (rag'ə·muf'in). Someone, especially a child, wearing rags.

rake. A man who leads a corrupt life.

rail (rāl). To use abusive, scornful language.

rank (rangk). Very vigorous and flourishing in growth, as vegetation; disagreeable to the taste or smell.

reconnoitering (rē'kə·noi'tər·ing). Examining and surveying for military purposes.

redoubtable (ri·dou'tə·bəl). Inspiring respect or fear.

respite (res'pit). Delay; interval of rest.

retribution (ret'rə·byŏŏ'shən). Punishment for wrongdoing.

ruck (ruk). Trash; rubbish.

sagacious (sə·gā'shəs). Wise.

sally (sal'ē). A joking remark or witticism.

PRONUNCIATION KEY: add, āce, câre, pälm; end, ēven; it, īce; odd, ōpen, ôrder; tŏŏk, pōōl; up, bûrn; ə = a in *above*, e in *sicken*, i in *flexible*, o in *melon*, u in *focus*; yŏŏ = u in *fuse*; oil; pout; check; ɡo; rinɡ; *th*in; *th*is; zh, vision.

salve (sav). Something that heals or soothes.

sardonic (sär·don'ik). Sneering.

sententious (sen·ten'shəs). Brief; formal.

sentient (sen'shē·ənt). Capable of feeling.

sepulchral (si·pul'krəl). Dismal; gloomy.

shibboleth (shib'ə·leth). A use of language distinctive of a social class.

shikepoke (shĭk'pok'). Night heron.

sluice (slo͞os). A trough through which water is run to separate gold from ore.

sojourn (sō'jûrn). Visit; a brief stay.

solstice (sol'stis). The time of the year when the sun is at its greatest distance from the equator, December 22 in winter and June 22 in summer.

sot. A drunkard.

spectral (spek'trəl). Ghostly.

stateroom. A private room on a passenger ship.

stentorian (sten·tor'ē·ən). Extremely loud.

stoic (stō'ik). One who is indifferent to pleasure and pain.

stolid (stol'id). Having or showing no emotion.

sublime (sə·blīm'). Grand; solemn; inspiring awe.

succumb (sə·kum'). To yield to force or persuasion.

tangible (tan'jə·bəl). Capable of being apprehended by the mind; real or material.

trammels (tram'əlz). Restraints.

transcendent (tran·sen'dənt). Extraordinary; of very high and remarkable degree.

transcient (tran'shənt). Short-lived; temporary.

trepidation (trep'ə·dā'shən). State of fear or alarm.

truculent (truk'yə·lənt). Harsh.

trundling (trund'ling). Rolling.

trysting (tris'ting) **place.** A meeting place for lovers.

unkempt (un·kempt'). Untidy; not clean and neat.

unobtrusive (un·əb·tro͞o'siv). Not tending to force or thrust oneself or one's opinions upon others.

unscathed (un·skāthd'). Uninjured.

urchin (ûr'chin). Mischievous boy.

vanquish (vang'kwish). Conquer.

vehement (ve'ə·mənt). Ardent; furious.

venomous (ven'əm·əs). Able to give a poisonous sting; spiteful.

verities (ver'ə·tēz). Truths; established principles.

vetch (vech). Beans grown for fodder.

viands (vī'əndz). Food.

vigilance (vij'ə·ləns). Alertness; watchfulness.

vindication (vin'də·kā'shən). Justification; proof of being right.

vindictive (vin·dik'tiv). Revengeful.

visage (viz'ij). Appearance, especially facial expression.

vituperative (vī·to͞o'pər·ə·tiv). Verbally abusive.

votary (vō'tər·ē). One devoted to a cause or vow; a worshiper.

waif (wāf). A homeless, neglected wanderer.

wag. A joker; a wit.

wary (war'ē). Carefully watchful; adv. *warily.*

wax. Increase; grow larger.

yokel (yō'kəl). Awkward person from the country (contemptuous term).

zealous (zel'əs). Enthusiastic.

zenith (zē'nith). The point in the sky that is directly overhead.

Index

A 0
B 1
C 2
D 3
E 4
F 5
G 6
H 7
I 8
J 9